Vocabulary Workout for the SSAT/ISEE

Volume I

Editorial:
Justin Grosslight, head author and editor.

First Edition, 2017

ISBN: 978-0-9984841-6-7

10 9 8 7 6 5 4 3 2 1

Vocabulary Workout for the SSAT/ISEE

Volume I

Justin Grosslight

Published by JJMG Enterprises LLC

Preface

Becoming an expert in any language is hard work. Regardless of whether English is your mother tongue, more advanced reading and vocabulary skills often accrue slowly and only with a sustained commitment to reading intricate material. Because of this, transitioning from communicating in popular English to becoming a consumer of scholarly and intellectual prose can be arduous work. While there is no supplement for reading erudite materials, building a vocabulary and an understanding of intellectual concepts is critical for language mastery.

In writing this edition of *Vocabulary Workout*, I had in mind the myriad individuals who are fluent in conversational English but who want to take their writing and vocabulary skills to the next level, especially those prepping for their SSAT and ISEE exams. Many of today's students and professionals seek to develop these skills, but find the task extraneous to their immediate needs, overly pedantic, or simply time consuming. *Vocabulary Workout* is meant to ease that process. Unlike other vocabulary books, many of which are merely extended word lists, this book is replete with exercises; there are also lessons to help you understand roots of words and intellectual terms. And the words are useful: they have been gleaned from statistical examination of SSAT and ISEE exams, which, in turn, excerpt their readings from a wide array of sophisticated prose materials.

These words are suitable for either classroom study or independent preparation. Do note, however, that the words in this book do not constitute an exhaustive vocabulary list necessary for success. This book is the first of two volumes used to help students prepare for their SSAT and ISEE exams. One can also purchase a complete edition of *Vocabulary Workout* that combines the contents of both volumes in one text.

Writing this book has been an evolving process, and I have enjoyed receiving feedback as it develops. In particular, I would like to thank Robert Fouldes, Nicoleta Marinescu, Tracy Nguyen, and Sonya Petkova for their contributions, sustained support, proofreading, and constructive criticism. Several students – Jack Le, Tram Huynh, Thanh Doan, Quoc Huynh, Tan Khoa, Trong Phan – have gladly provided input, corrected errors, and given frank suggestions as they used drafts of this book to prepare for their SSAT examinations. Marion Vangaeveren has done a fabulous job with the book's cover artwork.

I hope that this book will be as immensely useful to you as it has been for the students who have used it in its gestation period. With that said, good luck on your vocabulary endeavors!

Justin Grosslight

How to Use This Book

This book is intended to help build your vocabulary; it is a strategically organized catalogue of words that appear in intellectual and scholarly English, especially on secondary school entrance examinations. It is not, however, intended to be your sole source of learning words. Ideally, this book should be used in tandem with reading other scholarly and intellectual materials to help nurture your vocabulary growth.

Often to fully understand a word and its meaning(s), it is helpful to see a word in context many times. To reinforce this idea, the exercises contained in this book often require dictionary use. By looking up words in a dictionary, you can read samples of their uses in various settings and then apply what you have learned to the exercises in this text. Doing so will provide an active approach to building a vocabulary. This book's exercises also use a consistent intellectual vocabulary to complement the focal words of each lesson. Learning these words should further enhance your verbal skills.

At a stable pace, one should be able to absorb approximately fifty words, or ten lessons, per week. We have provided review quizzes after every ten lessons to help facilitate your study. One can study more words, of course, but diminishing returns may occur if more than twenty lessons are absorbed each week. Ideally this book should be studied at a moderate pace consistently over a long duration, allowing for time to let words sink in slowly. There are many more reasons why someone should use this book: whether you want to build a more solid vocabulary, you want to prepare for an examination, or you simply hope to sound erudite, all are good reasons for using this text. Whatever your purpose of study, however, it is imperative that you not give up on learning words.

Possessing a solid vocabulary can help you get in a good academic program, can make you more attractive for a corporate job, and can make you sound more articulate and knowledgeable. We hope you enjoy your endeavor to broaden your vocabulary with *Vocabulary Workout!*

TABLE OF CONTENTS

The Origins of English

English belongs to the family of Indo-European languages, which today comprise many languages spoken on the Earth. Most directly, the roots of English lay with Latin, the language of the Roman Empire that was spoken in the Mediterranean region two thousand years ago. From Latin emerged two families of European languages, Romance Languages and Germanic Languages. English is a Germanic language by structure and heritage, but also has borrowed much in style and vocabulary from French over the centuries (hence its proximity to French on the chart below). Many of the origins of English words stem from Latin, and still more come from Greek. The dashed line connecting Greek and Latin indicates that the languages had a cultural overlap, but that the former did not directly spawn the latter.

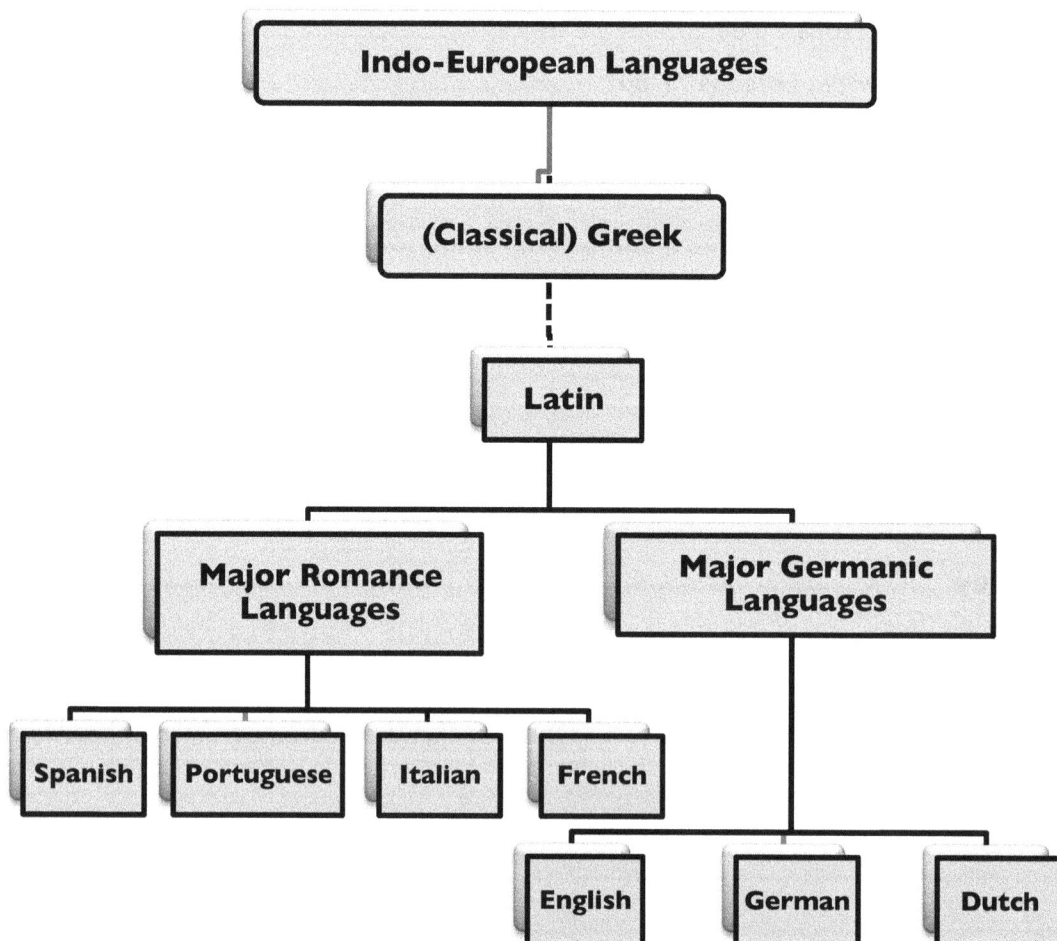

```
                    Indo-European Languages
                              |
                       (Classical) Greek
                              ┆
                            Latin
                     ┌────────┴────────┐
            Major Romance          Major Germanic
             Languages               Languages
         ┌────┬────┬────┐         ┌──────┬──────┐
      Spanish Portuguese Italian French  English German Dutch
```

In future sections we will explore techniques on how to decipher words you do not know. Often the best way to do this is to have an understanding of the roots of a word. Nearly all of the roots for English words come from Greek and Latin. As English became more globalized from the early modern era to today, it spread beyond its original confines of England thus borrowing and assimilating words from other languages. According to the Global Language Monitor, the English language contains over one million words and that number is growing. Though many such words are outmoded, over 170,000 are in current use. Luckily, to sound intellectual or scholarly, you only need to know a subset of these words.

NEW WORDS

elusive
i ˈlo͞osiv

impress
imˈpres

occupy
ˈäkyəˌpī

mettle
ˈmetl

derelict
ˈderəˌlikt

Lesson I

THE LOUSY BOSS

Most people thought Jordan was a terrible boss because he was so **elusive**. Not only was he **derelict** of his management duties at work, but he also would send memos filled with typos that failed to **impress** his employees. Because of these complications, workers at the company would **occupy** their time trying to figure out Jordan's whereabouts and the veracity of his credentials. For in the eyes of many, Jordan lacked the **mettle** to be a competent and effective superior.

Definitions: Try matching the words in the list with the appropriate definitions. If you are stuck, check the glossary in the back of the book or the passage at the top of the page.

1.   elusive   _____   a.   1. to make one feel admiration and respect; 2. to make a mark upon an object by using a stamp or seal; 3. to fix an idea in someone's mind

2.   impress   _____   b.   hard to find, catch, or achieve

3.   occupy   _____   c.   1. to reside or have one's business in; to be situated in; to fill or take up; to hold (a job); 2. (military) to enter, take control of, and remain in a place

4.   mettle   _____   d.   one's ability to manage a difficult situation in an enthusiastic and spirited way

5.   derelict   _____   e.   (adj.) in poor condition due to neglect and/or disuse; (n.) 1. a person lacking a job, home, or property; 2. a person negligent in doing his or her duty

Sentences: Try to use the words above in a sentence below. Remember that a word ending may be changed or its figure of speech slightly altered.

6.   I would like to move in and _____ the home on the beach.

7.   It is very hard to _____ a brilliant professor: one's work needs to be truly amazing to stand out.

8.   Jeremy was a(n) _____ person: it was difficult for people to locate him or for them to know his business plans and intentions.

9.   The new boss fired all the _____ in the company to keep costs down and increase efficiency.

10.   Yogya's _____ was tested when he had to prepare and pass his final exams as his poor father was dying.

3

Lesson 2

THE WOES OF A BUSINESSMAN

Despite his notable **generosity** to his family members, David would **urge** them to become more self-sufficient and not rely on his lucrative business for support. With his characteristic sharp and **pithy** remarks, David made it clear to them that they needed to stop complaining and to take financial action. David's sense of familial duty would often **compel** him to help his less entrepreneurial relatives; however, sometimes one could see the frustration in his eyes, even sadness and a certain **melancholy**: perhaps he just wished to be left alone.

NEW WORDS

urge
ərj

pithy
ˈpiTHē

generosity
ˌjenəˈräsitē

melancholy
ˈmelənˌkälē

compel
kəmˈpel

Definitions: Try matching the words in the list with the appropriate definitions. If you are stuck, check the glossary in the back of the book or the passage at the top of the page.

1.   urge   _____   a.   (n.) a strong desire or impulse; (v.) to try to persuade; to recommend strongly; to encourage (an animal or person) to move rapidly or in a certain direction

2.   pithy   _____   b.   to force or oblige someone or something; to bring about something by the use of pressure or force

3.   generosity _____   c.   (adj.) having or feeling sad and pensive; (n.) a feeling of sadness, typically with no apparent cause

4.   melancholy _____   d.   the quality of being kind, giving, and helpful

5.   compel   _____   e.   brief and forceful in expression

Sentences: Try to use the words above in a sentence below. Remember that a word ending may be changed or its figure of speech slightly altered.

6.   Janet had a(n) _____ feeling for a few weeks after her boyfriend of four years terminated the relationship.

7.   Often it is hard to _____ a lazy person to work hard and to achieve results.

8.   Barbara _____ her little cousin to study Spanish because she knew it would be an important global language in the future.

9.   In business, it is best to respond to emails in a(n) _____ manner rather than a longwinded one.

10.   Seth thanked all of his constituents for their _____ in supporting him in his bid to run for city mayor.

NEW WORDS

commodious
kəˈmōdēəs

obdurate
ˈäbd(y)ərit

paragon
ˈparəˌgän, -gən

languid
ˈlaNGgwid

flinch
flinCH

THE MAGNIFICENT MANSION

Many people believe that the mansion for sale on the hill is the **paragon** of elite living. Its rooms are **commodious**, providing plenty of room to sprawl out after a hard day's work. Its couches are large and soft – perfect for a **languid** person to doze throughout a relaxing afternoon. But when a rich stranger arrived from abroad and offered to buy the estate, its owner was **obdurate** and refused to negotiate. Rumors have it that the current owner did not even **flinch** when an offer was made for ten times the asking price.

Definitions: Try matching the words in the list with the appropriate definitions. If you are stuck, check the glossary in the back of the book or the passage at the top of the page.

1. commodious _____   a. roomy and comfortable

2. obdurate _____   b. 1. concerning a person, manner, or gesture showing a lack of exertion or effort; lacking energy; 2. a time period that's peaceful or pleasantly lazy

3. paragon _____   c. very stubbornly refusing to change one's opinion or course of action

4. languid _____   d. (n.) a fast, nervous movement of the body as an instinctive response to pain, surprise, or fear; (v.) to make a fast, nervous movement of the body as an instinctive response to pain, surprise, or fear

5. flinch _____   e. a person or thing regarded as the perfect example of something

Sentences: Try to use the words above in a sentence below. Remember that a word ending may be changed or its figure of speech slightly altered.

6. Nathan's little sister scolded him for being so _____: he refused to get off the couch and cook her lunch all afternoon.

7. If someone waves his or her hand very near my eyes, I am likely to _____.

8. Many people see Americans as a _____ of democracy and open-mindedness; nevertheless, America is still rife with problems.

9. The rooms in this house are so _____ that I feel I could stretch out almost anywhere.

10. Shareen was _____ and refused to compromise with her fiancé in choosing an appropriate wedding venue.

Lesson 4

FAMILY SECRETS

After the death of his parents, Patrick had to **assume** full responsibility for paying their **mortgage** and personal debts. Patrick's father had never been a financially successful man. During his last visit to the house, Patrick was surprised to come upon his father's diary, which was full of **elaborate** information about an overseas business venture. The discovery was enough to **whet** his curiosity and Patrick phoned his father's business partner. It turned out that Patrick's father had led a double life which neither Patrick nor his mother ever suspected. The old man was an **enigma** that Patrick was just beginning to uncover.

NEW WORDS

elaborate
iˈlab(ə)rit (adj.); iˈlabəˌrāt (v.)

mortgage
ˈmôrgij

assume
əˈso͞om

whet
(h)wet

enigma
iˈnigmə

Definitions: Try matching the words in the list with the appropriate definitions. If you are stuck, check the glossary in the back of the book or the passage at the top of the page.

1. elaborate _____ a. 1. to suppose to be the case without proof; 2. to take or begin to have power or responsibility; 3. to seize power or control over something; 4. to take on a characteristic or quality for a role

2. mortgage _____ b. a mystery

3. assume _____ c. 1. to acutely arouse someone's interest in something; 2. to sharpen the blade of an object (usually a knife)

4. whet _____ d. (n.) the charging of property (usually a home) by a debtor to a creditor as security for a debt; (v.) to convey property to a creditor as security on a loan

5. enigma _____ e. (adj.) 1. having many carefully arranged or designed details; detailed in plan or design; 2. lengthy and exaggerated; (v.) to add more detail concerning something already said

Sentences: Try to use the words above in a sentence below. Remember that a word ending may be changed or its figure of speech slightly altered.

6. Unlike June's writing, which is very _____, mine is concise and direct.

7. It is easy to _____ that Daysha hates pets since she has never owned one; in reality, however, she is allergic to animal fur.

8. Exactly how or why the British colony in Roanoke disappeared in around 1587 remains a(n) _____ to most historians.

9. An inspiring teacher can surely _____ one's interest in learning.

10. Most Americans take a(n) _____ to help them finance their home(s).

6

Lesson 5

WEDDING PLANNING

NEW WORDS

immaculate
iˈmakyəlit

obvious
ˈäbvēəs

invincible
inˈvinsəbəl

typical
ˈtipikəl

lavish
ˈlaviSH

It is **obvious** that weddings are important events in many peoples' lives. Because this is so, it is **typical** for an American bride and groom and their respective families to spend months planning the blessed event. Some families opt for very **lavish** weddings to be held at opulent estates or resort hotels, while others prefer a cozier, intimate event. But in either scenario, everyone hopes for an event that is **immaculate**. For at this time in a couple's lives, they often feel like they are **invincible** and that nothing in the world could tear them apart.

Definitions: Try matching the words in the list with the appropriate definitions. If you are stuck, check the glossary in the back of the book or the passage at the top of the page.

1. immaculate _____   a.   characteristic of a particular person, thing, group, era, or genre

2. obvious _____   b.   easily perceived or understood; easily apparent; self-evident; blatant

3. invincible _____   c.   too powerful to be overcome or defeated

4. typical _____   d.   1. perfectly neat or clean; 2. free of mistakes

5. lavish _____   e.   (adj.) extremely rich, luxurious, or elaborate; characterizing a person who is very generous or extravagant; given to profusion; (v.) to heap generous quantities upon

Sentences: Try to use the words above in a sentence below. Remember that a word ending may be changed or its figure of speech slightly altered.

6.   Most parents _____ excessive praise upon their children because they are proud of their offspring.

7.   Jamie is such an amazing basketball player that he seems _____: nobody can stand in his way or prevent him from scoring.

8.   It is _____ to me that the reason Jason's grades have not improved is because he never completes his homework assignments.

9.   It is _____ for a boy to ask a girl to dinner and a movie on a first date.

10.   After a long day of cleaning, one could say that our kitchen and living room looked _____.

Lesson 6

AN UNEXPECTED ENCOUNTER

The noise in the crowd rose to a **clamor**. He put his hands over his ears and closed his eyes. He was so tired of the same old speeches. Every new face seemed to be making the same obvious and **trite** remarks. Suddenly he felt as though someone was watching him. As if **telepathic**, he opened his eyes and sharply moved his body, causing him to **reel** backwards. He almost hit the person behind him. To his **delight**, the mysterious girl he had noticed before was standing there, smiling at him with a knowing glance, as if sharing his emotions.

NEW WORDS

clamor
ˈklamər

reel
rēl

telepathic
ˌteləˈpaTHik

delight
diˈlīt

trite
trīt

Definitions: Try matching the words in the list with the appropriate definitions. If you are stuck, check the glossary in the back of the book or the passage at the top of the page.

1. clamor _____ a. (n.) a cylinder upon which thread, film, wire, or other materials can be wound; (v.) to feel disoriented, bewildered, or off-kilter from a setback

2. reel _____ b. capable of transmitting thoughts to people without knowing their thoughts; psychic

3. telepathic _____ c. (n.) a loud and confused noise, perhaps protest; (v.) to shout loudly and insistently as a group, often to protest or demand

4. delight _____ d. concerning a remark, opinion, or idea that has lost its import and freshness due to overuse

5. trite _____ e. (n.) a great pleasure; (v.) to please (someone) greatly; to take great pleasure in something

Sentences: Try to use the words above in a sentence below. Remember that a word ending may be changed or its figure of speech slightly altered.

6. Troy could not immediately understand what the _____ outside his apartment was about: why were people protesting and what for?

7. Many clairvoyants claim to be _____ and to have direct communication with spirits or individuals of a higher power.

8. Often people make _____ remarks because they seem conventional rather than because they have any real import.

9. Ricardo was _____ when he received all "A"s on his report card.

10. Adriana was _____ after she heard that her cousin died in an automobile accident.

NEW WORDS

savor
ˈsāvər

premonition
ˌprēməˈniSHən, ˌprem-

token
ˈtōkən

lewd
lo͞od

repose
riˈpōz

The dirty old man had made a fortune on closing real estate deals and secretly cheating others in the process. Now, at the age of seventy, he thought he could **savor** his retirement. He called his **token** psychic to ask about his future, and she said she had a **premonition** that his life was about to fall apart. The following day, a woman filed a lawsuit against the man for making **lewd** comments about her at a videotaped gala earlier in the season. And one of the man's chief business rivals went to the media claiming that this old man led a life of **repose** rather than one of hard work. Suddenly the old man felt that enjoying his golden years was out of his grasp.

Definitions: Try matching the words in the list with the appropriate definitions. If you are stuck, check the glossary in the back of the book or the passage at the top of the page.

1. savor _____ a. an object serving as a visible or tangible representation of a fact; a characteristic or distinctive sign or mark of something

2. premonition _____ b. offensive and crude in a sexual way

3. token _____ c. to taste, drink, or enjoy something thoroughly and completely

4. lewd _____ d. (n.) a state of rest, sleep, or tranquility, composure; (v.) to be lying, sitting, or at rest in a particular place

5. repose _____ e. a strong feeling that something (typically unpleasant) is about to happen

Sentences: Try to use the words above in a sentence below. Remember that a word ending may be changed or its figure of speech slightly altered.

6. Maureen purchased a snow globe with the Manhattan skyline as a(n) _____ of her trip to New York.

7. Donald's _____ comments about women made his girlfriend feel uncomfortable.

8. Tram likes to _____ her favorite meals, so she eats very slowly and relishes the flavor of the great food.

9. Most people need some time for _____ after a long day's work.

10. I had a _____ that our business venture was going to fail when I noticed that my business partner quit coming to work every day.

Lesson 8

AN ANONYMOUS ACT OF KINDNESS

Jemma was a **precocious** child who could speak ten languages by the age of nine. Her language learning abilities were **unprecedented**. Naturally, Jemma wanted to enroll in college early; however, she was not able to afford it financially. But after Jemma showcased her abilities on a local television show, a **confidential** donor made a **pledge** of paying for half of for her higher education tuition. Jemma was deeply touched, and she knew she would always **cherish** the stranger's generous gesture.

NEW WORDS

cherish
ˈCHeriSH

confidential
ˌkänfəˈdenCHəl

pledge
plej

precocious
priˈkōSHəs

unprecedented
ˌənˈpresəˌdentid

Definitions: Try matching the words in the list with the appropriate definitions. If you are stuck, check the glossary in the back of the book or the passage at the top of the page.

1. cherish _____
2. confidential _____
3. pledge _____

    a. intended to be kept secret
    b. never done or known before
    c. (n.) 1. a solemn promise or understanding; 2. a promise of a donation to a charity; (v.) 1. to commit by solemn promise; 2. to formally declare or promise that something will be the case

4. precocious _____
5. unprecedented _____

    d. to protect and care for something or someone lovingly; to hold dear
    e. (of a child) having developed certain skills or abilities at an earlier age than usual; indicative of early development

Sentences: Try to use the words above in a sentence below. Remember that a word ending may be changed or its figure of speech slightly altered.

6. Vu _____ to be a responsible and faithful husband in his wedding vows.
7. The password to my safe box is _____ information not to be disclosed to strangers.
8. When Richard Nixon (1913-94) resigned as present on August 9, 1974, the event was _____: he became the first American leader to voluntarily depart office.
9. Alex is a (mathematically) _____ child: at the age of thirteen she is already learning twelfth grade math!
10. I _____ the time I spend with my cousins, as I rarely get to see them and my experiences with them are packed with meaning and memories.

NEW WORDS

conversation
ˌkänvərˈsāSHən

lax
laks

intriguing
inˈtrēgiNG

ruminate
ˈro͞oməˌnāt

calamity
kəˈlamitē

SPOILING CHILDREN

Often spoiling her son Jack with expensive gifts and seldom reprehending him for his mischief, Emily unknowingly turned Jack into a selfish and demanding bully. It was not until Jack seriously injured a friend when fighting over a toy that he found **intriguing** did Emily realize that he had gone too far. As she began to **ruminate** upon this **calamity**, and had a candid **conversation** with his teachers about Jack's misbehaviors, Emily realized that her **lax** parenting did more harm than good.

Definitions: Try matching the words in the list with the appropriate definitions. If you are stuck, check the glossary in the back of the book or the passage at the top of the page.

1.	conversation _____	a.	not strict, severe, or careful; loose; relaxed
2.	lax _____	b.	an informal exchange of ideas by spoken words
3.	intriguing _____	c.	arousing curiosity or interest; fascinating
4.	ruminate _____	d.	to think deeply about something
5.	calamity _____	e.	a disaster

Sentences: Try to use the words above in a sentence below. Remember that a word ending may be changed or its figure of speech slightly altered.

6.   Even though she is very famous today, I once had many _____ with Meghan and enjoyed our chats immensely.

7.   These seemingly _____ yet trivial matters can build up to become a major threat one day.

8.   I witnessed a _____ when two golf carts collided head on outside my kitchen window.

9.   Often teachers who are _____ cannot effectively compel their students to study when it is necessary.

10.   Often a course of action is more effective than spending time _____ on a matter.

Lesson 10

REVIVING THE ECONOMY

The new mayor gazed upon the **expanse** of the vineyards in front of him, hoping to **renovate** the economy of this fertile but nearly inaccessible region. Knowing that this region had a rich **heritage** of wine production, he wanted to extend its interregional **commerce** to the rest of the country. However, transporting the wine on the bad rural roads was a **tedious** and sometimes dangerous process. The mayor resolved to repair some of the main roads in order to facilitate the transportation process.

NEW WORDS

expanse
ikˈspans

tedious
ˈtēdēəs

heritage
ˈheritij

renovate
ˈrenəˌvāt

commerce
kəˈmens

Definitions: Try matching the words in the list with the appropriate definitions. If you are stuck, check the glossary in the back of the book or the passage at the top of the page.

1.	expanse	_____	a.	1. the act of buying and selling, trade; 2. social dealings between people
2.	tedious	_____	b.	to restore something old into a good state
3.	heritage	_____	c.	valued objects and qualities like cultural traditions, unsullied countryside, and historic buildings that have been passed down over generations current
4.	renovate	_____	d.	extremely long, slow, or dull; tiresome; monotonous
5.	commerce	_____	e.	an area of something that contains a wide and continuous surface; the distance to which something can stretch

Sentences: Try to use the words above in a sentence below. Remember that a word ending may be changed or its figure of speech slightly altered.

6.   Next week the restaurant will close to _____ its kitchen and seating areas; when it reopens, I imagine it will be more modern and in vogue.

7.   Allan found the task of writing an index for his book to be _____: associating words with page numbers for hours on end was extremely draining.

8.   If a nation places a trade embargo on another, _____ will cease to exist between the two countries.

9.   It is part of American _____ to eat turkey on Thanksgiving.

10.   The Sahara Desert covers a wide _____ of land in Northern Africa.

12

Word Search
Lessons 1-10

```
M N G T Y P I C A L B N Y M
E L E P M O C G T G O R N D
L E T A R U D B O I R L T M
A P R E M O N I T I O N C Z
N E E D G Z D A A S G I M G
C G L H R N S I S S H T H Y
H A B G S R I E U T S E R E
O G I P E I R U A G R U C R
L T C V L P R P G I N R M Y
Y R N R M E E T I E A P E
L O I I O L D A H M R U L R
C M V J E V G G M C C T E L
Z R N T K E A O E C Q E N N
R T I M K G C S O Z L B R I
```

1 (v.) 1. to make one feel admiration and respect; 2. to make a mark upon an object by using a stamp or seal; 3. to fix an idea in someone's mind

2 (v.) 1. to reside or have one's business in; to be situated in; to fill or take up; to hold (a job); 2. (military) to enter, take control of, and remain in a place

3 (adj.) having or feeling sad and pensive; (n.) a feeling of sadness, typically with no apparent cause

4 (v.) to force or oblige someone or something; to bring about something by the use of pressure or force

5 (adj.) stubbornly refusing to change one's opinion or course of action

6 (adj.) 1. concerning a person, manner, or gesture showing a lack of exertion

7 (n.) the charging of property (usually a home) by a debtor to a creditor as security for a debt; (v.) to convey property to a creditor as security on a loan

8 (v.) 1. to suppose to be the case without proof; 2. to take or begin to have power or responsibility; 3. to seize power or control over something; 4. to take on a characteristic or quality for a role

9 (adj.) too powerful to be overcome or defeated

10 (adj.) characteristic of a particular person, thing, group, era, or genre

11 (n.) a cylinder upon which thread, film, wire, or other materials can be wound; (v.) to feel disoriented, bewildered, or off-kilter from a setback

12 (adj.) capable of transmitting thoughts to people without knowing their thoughts; psychic

13 (v.) to taste, drink, or enjoy something thoroughly and completely

14 (n.) a strong feeling that something (typically unpleasant) is about to happen

15 (v.) to protect and care for something or someone lovingly; to hold dear

16 (n.) 1. a solemn promise or understanding; 2. a promise of a donation to a charity; (v.) 1. to commit by solemn promise; 2. to formally declare or promise that something will be the case

17 (n.) an informal exchange of ideas by spoken words

18 (adj.) arousing curiosity or interest; fascinating

19 (n.) valued objects and qualities like cultural traditions, unsullied countryside, and historic buildings that have been passed down over generations

20 (v.) 1. the act of buying and selling, trade; 2. social dealings between people

Vocabulary Review
Lessons 1-10

Directions: Match each word with its best approximate definition. Note that definitions are not necessarily repeated verbatim from the lesson exercises.

1.	elusive	_____	a.	never done or known before
2.	mettle	_____	b.	concise and forcefully expressive
3.	pithy	_____	c.	to restore (usually a building) to be in a good state or tasteful
4.	generosity	_____	d.	spotless; flawless
5.	commodious	_____	e.	a state of rest, sleep, or tranquility
6.	paragon	_____	f.	a mystery
7.	whet	_____	g.	a person or thing regarded as the perfect example of something
8.	enigma	_____	h.	easily perceived or understood; clear; blatant
9.	immaculate	_____	i.	to think deeply about something
10.	obvious	_____	j.	intended to be kept either private or secret
11.	delight	_____	k.	to please someone greatly
12.	trite	_____	l.	concerning a remark, opinion, or Idea that is overused and thus of very little import
13.	lewd	_____	m.	not sufficiently strict, severe, or careful
14.	repose	_____	n.	to excite or stimulate; to sharpen
15.	confidential	_____	o.	the quality of being kind and willing to give
16.	unprecedented	_____	p.	crude and offensive in a sexual way
17.	lax	_____	q.	hard to catch or grasp
18.	ruminate	_____	r.	a person's ability to cope well with difficulties
19.	tedious monotonous	_____	s.	too long, dull, or slow;
20.	renovate	_____	t.	roomy and spacious

Introduction to Word Roots

As we have seen, many of the origins of English come from (Classical) Greek and Latin. Though these languages are defunct today, English contains a number of words with roots whose derivatives stem from these languages.

Consider, for example the (Classical) Greek word $\varphi\acute{o}\beta o\varsigma$, or phobos. Translated into English as "phobia" or "phobe," this word means "fear." While (Classical) Greek is no longer an active language, the root "phobia" persists in English language to describe an extreme irrational fear of something. Consider the following examples:

agora<u>phobia</u> (<u>n.</u>):   extreme irrational fear of large crowded places

arachno<u>phobia</u> (<u>n.</u>):   extreme irrational fear of spiders

techno<u>phobe</u> (<u>n.</u>):   a person who is afraid of or who dislikes technology

xeno<u>phobia</u> (<u>n.</u>):   extreme irrational fear of people from other countries

Just as was so with (Classical) Greek, English has words whose root derive from Latin. Consider, for example, the Latin word *placere*, meaning to please. Certain English words containing "plac" are related to the concept of pleasing someone or something:

<u>plac</u>ate (v.):   to make less angry or hostile

im<u>plac</u>able (adj.):   unable to be pleased or appeased (note that the root "im" means "not" and is taught in our first word root lesson)

Roots, therefore, can help us decipher potential meanings of words without knowing exactly what a word means. Note, however, that not every word has roots, nor does a word that contains letters that look like a root imply that the word is related to its root meaning. The word "<u>plac</u>ard" refers to a poster or sign used in public display, which has nothing to do with pleasing anyone. In this book, we provide you with a number of units to help you identify and practice identifying word roots.

Word Roots: Unit 1

ROOTS AND THEIR MEANINGS

In/il/im/ir:	not	chron:	time
ex/ej:	out	a:	without
re:	again	morph:	shape

Here are a few examples of some words that use the above roots:

intolerable:	not tolerable
illegal:	not legal
improper:	not proper
incapable:	not capable
irrational:	not rational
exit:	(place) to go out
eject:	to force or throw out
chronology:	telling a story where events are arranged in order of their occurrence
amorphous:	having no definite shape

Now try to fill in the table below by finding the appropriate root(s) and interpreting the meaning of each word:

Word	Root(s)	Guessed Meaning	Actual Meaning
inaccurate			
incapable			
illegitimate			
impolite			
inactive			
excrete			
chronicle			
morphology			
asexual			

atypical			
anachronism			
irreverent			
apolitical			
inexplicable			

Remember that not every group of letters forming a root implies that there is a root for a given word. Consider, for example, the word "apple." One may think that the "a" in apple means not, but the "a" is merely a letter. Also the word "real" has "re" in the beginning, but it has nothing to do with doing something again. Roots, therefore, are only tools to help *possibly* identify the meaning of a word if you are completely stuck.

Occupations and Careers I

As you learn more advanced English, you will be exposed to many papers that discuss what different scholars, intellectuals, or professionals do in their careers. Knowing what people in different careers do is helpful for understanding the gist of many pieces of writing. Furthermore, people in these careers are discussed frequently on school entrance examinations. The list of occupational roles below and in the next section is not exhaustive, but rather is an attempt to help define a number of specific and sophisticated occupations to which you may be exposed to or read about as an intellectual.

SCIENTIFIC JOBS

anatomist:
one who practices anatomy, e.g. the body structures of humans and other living creatures, often through dissection to examine their innards

astronomer:
one who practices astronomy, e.g. celestial objects, space, and the physical universe as a whole

biologist:
one who practices biology, e.g. living organisms, their morphology, physiology, anatomy, behavior, and distribution

botanist:
one who practices botany, e.g. plants, their physiology, structure, genetics, ecology, distribution, classification, and economic importance

chemist:
one who practices chemistry, e.g. chemicals and their reactions

geneticist:	one who practices genetics, e.g. heredity and the variation of inherited characteristics through genes
geologist:	one who practices geology, e.g. Earth's physical structure and composition, its history, and forces that affect it
meteorologist:	one who practices meteorology, e.g. the study of the atmosphere and the weather
oceanographer:	one who practices oceanography, e.g. the physical and biological processes of the seas
paleontologist:	one who practices paleontology, e.g. the fossil elements of animals and plants
physicist:	one who practices physics, e.g. the study of the nature and properties of matter and energy
seismologist:	one who practices seismology, e.g., the science of earthquakes and related incidents
zoologist:	one who practices zoology, e.g. the behavior, structure, distribution, and classification of animals

MEDICAL OR MEDICALLY RELATED JOBS

anesthesiologist:	one who practices anesthesia, e.g. administering gases or drugs to make patients insensitive to pain before surgical operations
coroner:	an official who investigates deaths, especially violent or suspicious deaths

hygienist:	**specialist who promotes sanitary conditions to maintain good health**
pharmacist:	**specialist who is professionally qualified to prepare and dispense drugs**
surgeon:	**one who practices surgery, e.g. the treatment of the body through incision and manipulation**
veterinarian:	**a doctor and surgeon for animals**

NEW WORDS

din
din

zany
ˈzānē

clairvoyant
kle(ə)rˈvoiənt

ethical
ˈeTHikəl

withstand
wiTHˈstand, wiTH-

Lesson 11

FROM CONSTRUCTION TO CORRUPT PROGNOSTICATION

Noah could no longer **withstand** going to work and operating a crane every day. He detested the monotony of the job and especially loathed the **din** made by bulldozers and cement trucks at the construction site. So he chose to quit his job in pursuit of a rather **zany** adventure: he wanted to be a seer. Not knowing how to commence with this task, he sought out a local **clairvoyant** and solicited her advice. In confidence, she urged him not to be **ethical** and to do everything he could to prey on his clients' weaknesses in order to take as much money as possible from them. Thus began Noah's corrupt career in prognostication.

Definitions: Try matching the words in the list with the appropriate definitions. If you are stuck, check the glossary in the back of the book or the passage at the top of the page.

1. din _____ a. (adj.) having the ability to see or predict events in the future beyond normal sense; (n.) a person who claims to have the supernatural ability to see events in the future beyond normal sense

2. zany _____ b. of or relating to moral principles; morally correct

3. clairvoyant _____ c. amusingly unconventional and idiosyncratic

4. ethical _____ d. to remain undisturbed or unaffected by something, to resist; to offer strong resistance or opposition to

5. withstand _____ e. a loud, unpleasant, and prolonged noise

Sentences: Try to use the words above in a sentence below. Remember that a word ending may be changed or its figure of speech slightly altered.

6. Simon is a strong person; he is able to _____ intense criticism about his work habits and still can succeed in his career.

7. Elizabeth has the _____ notion of planting plastic flowers instead of real ones on her property because they would require less upkeep.

8. Most fortunetellers claim to possess _____ powers.

9. It is not _____ to cheat in an exam.

10. The machines paving the road outside my home created a protracted _____, thus making it difficult to concentrate.

Lesson 12

MANAGEMENT TRANSITION FEARS

As vice president of the company, Rynna worried that the business may not **flourish** when the CEO resigns in December. After all, it was the CEO's dedication and charisma that gave the company a rich and effective **texture**. Rynna, along with other top executives, worried that the employees would begin to work at a **sedate** pace in the absence of the CEO, thus hindering productivity and profits. Executive discussions also transpired about whether to **poach** a top executive from a competitor company. Because the ultimate decision was not to steal an executive competitor, Rynna told herself that she must metaphorically **fasten** her seat belt and prepare for a very turbulent corporate ride during its transition state.

Definitions: Try matching the words in the list with the appropriate definitions. If you are stuck, check the glossary in the back of the book or the passage at the top of the page.

1.	sedate	_____	a.	calm, dignified, and unhurried; quiet and dull
2.	texture	_____	b.	the feel, quality, or appearance of a substance or surface; the quality created by a combination of elements in a musical or literary work
3.	fasten	_____	c.	1. to illegally hunt or catch; 2. to acquire in a secretive way
4.	poach	_____	d.	to close or join securely; to fix in place; to fix one's attention on something
5.	flourish	_____	e.	(n.) an elaborate literary or rhetorical expression; (v.) for a person or other living organism to grow in a healthy or vigorous way, usually as the result of a favorable environment

Sentences: Try to use the words above in a sentence below. Remember that a word ending may be changed or its figure of speech slightly altered.

6. It is important to _____ your seatbelt when you drive a car.
7. Adding hot pepper sauce sauce to ice cream not only seems unpalatable, but it also changes the _____ of the food, making it taste grainy rather than smooth.
8. In order for a child to _____, it is necessary to provide that child with a strong and stable environment.
9. Medicine was used to _____ Long, who is typically energetic and hyper, before the surgery.
10. Often teams _____ athletes from competing teams in order to enhance their status and competitiveness.

NEW WORDS

judge
jəj

tome
tōm

procure
prəˈkyŏŏr, prō-

invariable
inˈve(ə)rēəbəl

subsist
səbˈsist

Lesson 13

THE MATH PROFESSOR

The math professor had never seen an argument like this before, so he told his doctoral student that he was unfit to **judge** whether the research was sound until he conducted further research. In doing so, the professor aimed to **procure** a **tome** of algebraic research that discussed theories similar to the one that his student had presented. But the book the professor sought was hard to acquire, and the professor had to **subsist** on his intellect alone until the text arrived. After doing further research, the professor concluded that his student's argument was valid and brilliant. From that point on, he had **invariable** support for the student who presented this work.

Definitions: Try matching the words in the list with the appropriate definitions. If you are stuck, check the glossary in the back of the book or the passage at the top of the page.

1. judge _____ a. (n.) an individual with the authority to decide cases in courts of law; an individual who decides the results of competition or infractions of rules; (v.) 1. to form an opinion or conclusion about; 2. to decide a case in court; 3. to decide the results of a competition

2. tome _____ b. unchanging

3. procure _____ c. to maintain or support oneself, generally at a minimal level

4. invariable _____ d. a book, particularly one that is large, heavy, and scholarly

5. subsist _____ e. to obtain something, usually with effort

Sentences: Try to use the words above in a sentence below. Remember that a word ending may be changed or its figure of speech slightly altered.

6. I am not a good _____ of whether this wine is of high quality because I rarely drink.

7. Stranded in the woods on a camping trip, the boys were forced to _____ on only water and crackers for three days.

8. Paula's dissertation was a _____: she wrote over five hundred pages about plant collecting in early modern Italy.

9. A good spouse will be _____ committed to his or her partner.

10. It is difficult for Americans to _____ durians because not many grocers wish to stock the smelly and exotic Southeast Asian fruit.

23

Lesson 14

THE MEDICAL INTERVIEW

While waiting in the **antechamber** to the interview room, Alex felt his courage **wane**. The traditional medical (Aesculapian) **symbol** on the wall of a staff and snakes suddenly scared him. Alex had always been sure that he wanted to become a medical doctor. His father was a famous physician who had invested an **abundant** amount of money and effort into Alex' education. Destiny seemed to be determined for Alex from a young age; all he had to do was **cooperate**. All of a sudden, for the first time in his life, Alex felt overwhelmed by an uncomfortable feeling of doubt.

Definitions: Try matching the words in the list with the appropriate definitions. If you are stuck, check the glossary in the back of the book or the passage at the top of the page.

1.	symbol	_____	a.	existing or available in great quantities
2.	antechamber	_____	b.	a thing that represents or stands for something else, especially a material object that stands for something else
3.	abundant	_____	c.	to decrease in vigor or power; to recede; to ebb
4.	cooperate	_____	d.	to act jointly and work toward the same end; to assist someone (or an organization) and comply with his or her (its) requests
5.	wane	_____	e.	a small room leading to a big one

Sentences: Try to use the words above in a sentence below. Remember that a word ending may be changed or its figure of speech slightly altered.

6. Uriah waited in the _____ for his host to lead him into the conference room.

7. Bananas are generally _____ in tropical forests, as trees which grow them are numerous.

8. I am waiting to swim until the tide _____.

9. Even though they are siblings, Sherry and Meryl have difficulty trying to _____ on team projects.

10. A heart is a(n) _____ that is used to stand for love.

NEW WORDS

tempt
tem(p)t

lament
lə'ment

rotund
rō'tənd, 'rō͵tənd

elocution
͵elə'kyoōSHən

extrapolate
ik'strapə͵lāt

Lesson 15

THE TRIAL

A master of **elocution**, James vividly described the scene to the jury who seemed to be mesmerized by his charismatic voice and **rotund** physique. They seemed to be moved by his **lament** for the lack of love and attention that his late wife had expressed towards him. James knew he could **tempt** them to see him as the emotional victim of a dysfunctional, abusive relationship. From his heartfelt story and soft manner of speaking, it was very difficult to **extrapolate** any proof that he might have been an aggressor.

Definitions: Try matching the words in the list with the appropriate definitions. If you are stuck, check the glossary in the back of the book or the passage at the top of the page.

1. tempt _____   a.   the skill of articulate and expressive speech
2. lament _____   b.   to entice; to allure; to try to entice one to do something that he or she finds attractive but that he or she also knows is wrong
3. rotund _____   c.   to extend the application of a method or a conclusion to an unknown trend by assuming that existing trends will continue or that similar methods will be applicable
4. elocution _____   d.   plump; round or spherical
5. extrapolate _____   e.   (n.) 1. a passionate expression of grief or sorrow; 2. a song or poem expressing sorrow; 3. an expression of disappointment; (v.) to mourn a person's death

Sentences: Try to use the words above in a sentence below. Remember that a word ending may be changed or its figure of speech slightly altered.

6. Howard looked positively _____ after putting on fifty pounds last year.
7. A good speaker delivers a speech with excellent _____ and thus moves his or her audience.
8. Sara _____ the fact that she chose not to finish college and worried that it was too late to return for her degree.
9. Jake _____ me to visit his new restaurant by offering me a free meal.
10. Physicists often must _____ upon their data to come up with sound hypotheses.

Lesson 16

THE RIGHT FIT

While never being on the skinny side, Jeffrey had always managed to maintain a good figure. In spite of his efforts, however, Jeffrey felt himself becoming quite **corpulent** at the end of the holiday season. His chest was **heaving** with increasingly more difficult breaths and his **sturdy** stomach was bulging out grotesquely. "It is **essential** that I **rescind** the contract I made with my weight loss agency," Jeffrey thought to himself. "Being under a contractual obligation to lose weight seems to have had the exact opposite effect for me," he concluded.

NEW WORDS

corpulent
ˈkôrpyələnt

rescind
riˈsind

essential
iˈsenCHəl

sturdy
ˈstərdē

heave
hēv

Definitions: Try matching the words in the list with the appropriate definitions. If you are stuck, check the glossary in the back of the book or the passage at the top of the page.

1. corpulent _____ a. (n.) a push, haul, or throw requiring great effort; (v.) 1. to push, haul, or throw with great effort; 2. to produce a sigh

2. rescind _____ b. strong and solidly built; showing resistance and determination

3. essential _____ c. to revoke, cancel, or appeal (a law, order, or judgment)

4. sturdy _____ d. absolutely necessary; extremely important

5. heave _____ e. fat (describing a person)

Sentences: Try to use the words above in a sentence below. Remember that a word ending may be changed or its figure of speech slightly altered.

6. It is _____ to get eight hours of sleep each day if you want to function properly.

7. Nancy tried to _____ Mark's marriage proposal after she discovered that Mark had been lying to her during their courtship.

8. One final _____ should push the piano up the ramp and into our foyer.

9. Unlike the wobbly old table, this one appears to be much more _____.

10. Helga was so _____ that she needed two airplane seats instead of one to support her body.

NEW WORDS

generate
ˈjenəˌrāt

astound
əˈstound

gimmick
ˈgimik

captivating
ˈkaptəˌvātiNG

eventual
iˈvenCHo͞oəl

Lesson 17

TO CAPTIVATE AN AUDIENCE

The journalist knew that the new debate show was just another **gimmick** to **generate** interest among ordinary citizens. Television producers claimed that they would **astound** the audience with a **captivating** show that supposedly presented new and unusual perspectives. However, the journalist could immediately see that the same old political views were hidden behind the new glossy cover. He was aware that the hype would wear off very quickly and that viewers would experience **eventual** disappointment with the new show.

Definitions: Try matching the words in the list with the appropriate definitions. If you are stuck, check the glossary in the back of the book or the passage at the top of the page.

1.   generate   _____   a.   to produce; to cause a particular situation or emotion to come about
2.   astound   _____   b.   occurring at the end or as a result of a sequence of events; ultimate; final
3.   gimmick   _____   c.   a device or trick aimed at attracting attention, publicity, or business
4.   captivating _____   d.   to shock or greatly surprise
5.   eventual   _____   e.   capable of attracting and holding interest

Sentences: Try to use the words above in a sentence below. Remember that a word ending may be changed or its figure of speech slightly altered.

6.   The physics professor's lecture this morning was so _____ that I suddenly felt inspired to pursue a doctorate after I graduate.
7.   I was _____ when I heard that my cousin Trevor possessed a winning lottery ticket.
8.   Smoking and drinking led to Isidor's _____ and tragic demise.
9.   It can be hard to _____ innovative ideas because there are myriad people and conceptions already in existence.
10.   Many businesses use advertising _____ to try and procure clientele.

Lesson 18

THE SADISTIC HUSBAND

The wife repeatedly reminded her husband of his household responsibilities, but the old **sluggard** refused to move from the couch. In his view, his wife was supposed to be **submissive** to him and follow his orders – not the other way around. He could not **relinquish** his control over her or his love for spending endless hours in front of the television. In fact, her pleas would **entice** him to act in an even more **tyrannical** manner. He derived pleasure from deriding her and making her feel powerless.

Definitions: Try matching the words in the list with the appropriate definitions. If you are stuck, check the glossary in the back of the book or the passage at the top of the page.

1.	sluggard _____	a.	to voluntarily give up
2.	submissive _____	b.	a lazy person
3.	entice _____	c.	to attract or tempt by offering pleasure or advantage
4.	relinquish _____	d.	exercising power in an arbitrary or cruel way
5.	tyrannical _____	e.	ready to conform to the commands or will of others

Sentences: Try to use the words above in a sentence below. Remember that a word ending may be changed or its figure of speech slightly altered.

6. Ellie's uncharacteristic _____ behavior terrified her childhood friends, who remembered her as a cooperative and sensitive person.

7. The dictator refused to _____ his power; only with a coup was he deposed and peace reinstated in our homeland.

8. Parents often try to _____ their children to study in school by rewarding them with money or presents for obtaining good grades.

9. Quinn is a(n) _____ when it comes to work: rarely is she on time and it takes much effort to get her off of her couch and engaged with customers.

10. Too often people are _____ to their superiors and avoid expressing themselves in a candid, creative manner.

NEW WORDS

focus
ˈfōkəs

detail
diˈtāl, ˈdētāl

potent
ˈpōtnt

tolerate
ˈtälə͵rāt

ridicule
ˈridi͵kyo͞ol

THE BAD PORTRAIT PAINTER

Even though he was middle aged, Vincent hoped that he would one day become a famous portrait painter. Unfortunately, he was subject to **potent ridicule** by his coworkers for articulating this dream. Looking at his work, they laughed at his inability to **focus** on any **detail** of a person's face. His painting was so terrible, they said, that one could hardly distinguish between a nose and an ear. Vincent would often endure spells of depression after receiving such criticism. But he eventually learned to **tolerate** their criticism. While he never became famous, Vincent continued to create many mediocre works before he retired from pursuing art.

Definitions: Try matching the words in the list with the appropriate definitions. If you are stuck, check the glossary in the back of the book or the passage at the top of the page.

1.   focus   _____   a.   (n.) the subjection of someone or something to contemptuous or dismissive language or behavior; (v.) to subject someone or something to contemptuous and dismissive language or behavior

2.   detail   _____   b.   having great power, influence, or effect

3.   potent   _____   c.   to allow the existence, practice, or occurrence of something; to be able to withstand something, to endure or accept

4.   tolerate   _____   d.   (n.) 1. the center of interest or activity; 2. the state or quality of having or producing clear visual definition; (v.) 1. to adapt to the prevailing level of light so as to see clearly; 2. to pay attention to (focus on)

5.   ridicule   _____   e.   (n.) an individual feature, fact, or item; (v.) to give particulars of, describe item by item

Sentences: Try to use the words above in a sentence below. Remember that a word ending may be changed or its figure of speech slightly altered.

6.   Art hated being _____ by the class bully and got his principal involved.

7.   It is important to _____ on achieving goals; otherwise, one can be distracted and not accomplish as much or as quickly.

8.   A surgeon must pay great attention to _____, for if he or she is only slightly off in an operation, a patient's life may be jeopardized.

9.   Indian restaurants often possess a(n) _____, distinctive smell of curry.

10.   Learning to _____ differences in other people helps individuals get along better with their peers.

Lesson 20

UNCOMFORTABLE MEMORIES

The **reminiscence** of his turbulent early days would often come to him unexpectedly, in a **stealthy** manner like a thief. The violent and erratic behavior of his gang had caused **mayhem** in his childhood neighborhood. He had become notorious for his cruelty and anger even among his friends. He was older now and understood that his previous actions were nothing to **commend**. He wished that he could undo all the madness that he had caused; however, there was no way to fix the past.

Definitions: Try matching the words in the list with the appropriate definitions. If you are stuck, check the glossary in the back of the book or the passage at the top of the page.

1.	reminiscence _____	a.	famous or well-known, especially for a bad deed or quality
2.	stealthy _____	b.	a story or recollection of past events
3.	mayhem _____	c.	to praise formally or officially; to present as suitable for approval or acceptance; recommend
4.	commend _____	d.	behavior done in a surreptitious manner so as to not be seen or heard
5.	notorious _____	e.	damaging or violent disorder; chaos

Sentences: Try to use the words above in a sentence below. Remember that a word ending may be changed or its figure of speech slightly altered.

6. Most thieves need to be _____ in their operation so that they are not caught.

7. Great _____ ensued after a great earthquake demolished large swaths of greater Kathmandu.

8. The _____ German politician Adolf Hitler (1889-1945) exterminated over six million Jews in German concentration camps during World War II.

9. Astrid _____ her little sister for her hard work and efforts in the school talent show.

10. Marco's latest book contained many _____ from his early childhood in Catalonia.

Crossword Puzzle
Lessons 11-20

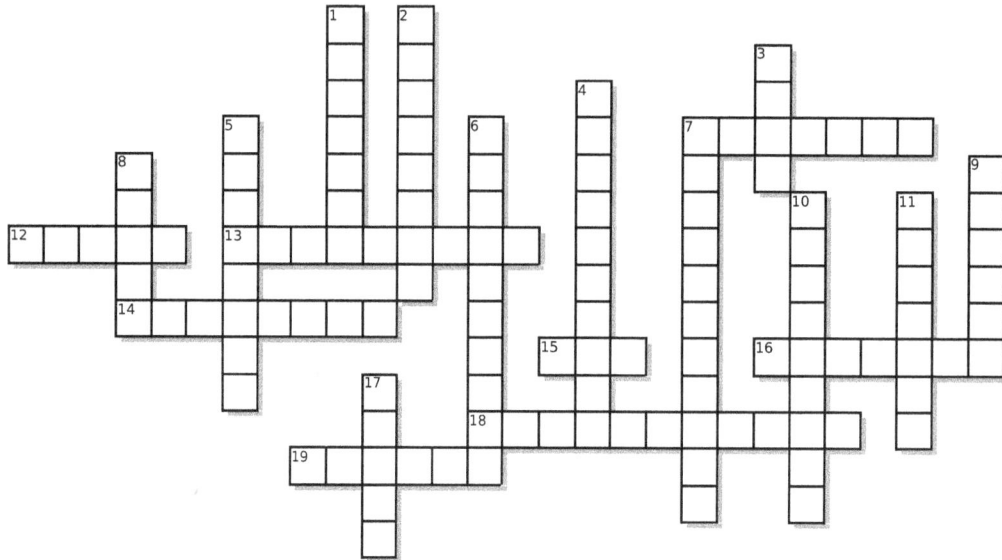

ACROSS

7 (v.) to praise formally or officially; to present as suitable for approval or acceptance; recommend
12 (v.) 1. to illegally hunt or catch; 2. to acquire in a secretive way
13 (adj.) absolutely necessary; extremely important
14 (adj.) behavior done in a surreptitious manner so as to not be seen or heard
15 (n.) a loud, unpleasant, and prolonged noise
16 (v.) to maintain or support oneself, generally at a minimal level
18 (n.) a small room leading to a big one
19 (n.) a thing that represents or stands for something else, especially a material object that stands for something else

DOWN

1 (n.) the feel, quality, or appearance of a substance or surface; the quality created by a combination of elements in a musical or literary work
2 (v.) to allow the existence, practice, or occurrence of something; to be able to withstand something, to endure or accept
3 (n.) a book, particularly one that is large, heavy, and scholarly
4 (adj.) ready to conform to the commands or will of others
5 (v.) to produce; to cause a particular situation or emotion to come about
6 (adj.) exercising power in an arbitrary or cruel way
7 (adj.) having the ability to see or predict events in the future beyond normal sense; (n.) a person who claims to have the supernatural ability to see events in the future beyond normal sense
8 (n.) 1. the center of interest or activity; 2. the state or quality of having or producing clear visual definition; (v.) 1. to adapt to the prevailing level of light so as to see clearly; 2. to pay attention to (focus on)
9 (n.) 1. a passionate expression of grief or sorrow; 2. a song or poem expressing sorrow; 3. an expression of disappointment; (v.) to mourn a person's death
10 (adj.) fat (describing a person)
11 (n.) a device or trick aimed at attracting attention, publicity, or business
17 (v.) to entice; to allure; to try to entice one to do something that he or she finds attractive but that he or she also knows is wrong

Vocabulary Review
Lessons 11-20

Directions: Match each word with its best approximate definition. Note that definitions are not necessarily repeated verbatim from the lesson exercises.

1.	zany	_____	a.	strong and solidly built
2.	ethical	_____	b.	existing or available in large quantities; plentiful
3.	sedate	_____	c.	a lazy or torpid person
4.	fasten	_____	d.	the recollection of past events
5.	procure	_____	e.	to close or join securely; to fix or hold in place
6.	invariable	_____	f.	round or spherical (of a person)
7.	abundant	_____	g.	to tempt or attract by offering pleasure or advantage
8.	wane	_____	h.	amusingly unconventional and idiosyncratic
9.	rotund	_____	i.	having great power, influence, or effect
10.	elocution	_____	j.	morally good or correct
11.	rescind	_____	k.	to calm someone, typically by administering a drug
12.	sturdy	_____	l.	an individual feature, fact, or item
13.	astound	_____	m.	to obtain
14.	captivating	_____	n.	capable of attracting and holding interest
15.	sluggard	_____	o.	to revoke, cancel, or appeal (a law or agreement)
16.	entice	_____	p.	to shock or greatly surprise
17.	detail	_____	q.	to decrease in vigor, power, or extent
18.	potent	_____	r.	chaos; violent or damaging disorder
19.	reminiscence	_____	s.	never changing
20.	mayhem	_____	t.	the skill of articulate and expressive speech

Word Roots: Unit 2

ROOTS AND THEIR MEANINGS

ante:	before	pre:	before
loc/loq/log:	to speak	bi/di:	two
sci:	to know	bene:	good
sub:	under, less than	inter:	between, among

Here are a few examples of some words that use the above roots:

antedate:
to date before something; to come before something else in time

loquacious:
talkative

science
the study of how the world works (biologically, chemically, physically or otherwise); knowing about the world through these properties

predecease:
to die before someone or something

subordinate:
lower in rank or position; to work under someone

benefit:
an advantage

bicycle:
a pedal-powered vehicle with two wheels

interstate:
existing or carried between states

Now try to fill in the table below by finding the appropriate root(s) and interpreting the meaning of each word:

Word	Root(s)	Guessed Meaning	Actual Meaning
antecedent			
subservient			
eloquent			
prescient			
beneficial			
predecessor			
dialogue			
interlocutor			
biweekly			

subway			
internecine			
benediction			
dichotomy			
submissive			
conscience			
predetermined			

Occupations and Careers II

This section continues the list of occupations and careers from the previous section. As before, we have broken them up by field.

SOCIAL SCIENCE RELATED JOBS

anthropologist: one who practices anthropology, e.g. the study of humankind, its culture, its development, or its evolution and ecology

cartographer: one who practices cartography, e.g. the practice of drawing maps

demographer: one who practices demography, e.g. the study of births, deaths, income, and other structural elements of human populations

psychiatrist: one who practices psychiatry, e.g. one with whom one can discuss personal, mental, and social problems; unlike a psychologist a psychiatrist can prescribe medication to help a patient

psychologist: one who practices psychology, e.g. the study of the mind and emotions that govern behavior in specific contexts; a therapist with whom one can discuss personal, mental, and social problems

sociologist: one who practices sociology, e.g. the study of social problems relative to the structure, development, and functioning of human society

JOBS IN THE LEGAL FIELD

bailiff: an official of the court who keeps order, looks after prisoners, executes writs, and carries out arrests

criminologist: one who practices criminology, e.g. the study of crime and criminals

magistrate: a civil officer or lay judge who administers the law for minor offenses or for screening of larger offenses

POLITICAL JOBS

governor: the elected head of a state in the United States; the title of the head of a colony in British colonies

mayor: someone elected head of a town, city, or other designated municipality

representative: (1) someone who serves in the United States House of Representatives; (2) a person (often legally) elected to speak on behalf of a group and imbued with legislative power

senator: someone who serves on the United States Senate

NEW WORDS

divulge
di'vəlj, dī-

gouge
gouj

barren
'barən

liberty
'libərtē

repulse
ri'pəls

Lesson 21

THE PRIVILEGED STUDENT

Two boys got into a fight last week: Martin tried to **gouge** out the eye of his rival, Baron. He was angry that Baron would not **divulge** the name of the boy who scratched his car. Martin could not believe that anyone would take the **liberty** to do such a thing. He knew he could not **repulse** all the hatred towards him for being the richest boy in the school. At the same time, Martin was also convinced that all the boys' attempts to destabilize him were **barren**: his father owned the school and the teachers would do whatever he wanted of them.

Definitions: Try matching the word in the box with the appropriate definition. If you are stuck, check the glossary in the back of the book or the passage at the top of the page.

1.	divulge	_____	a.	to make private or sensitive information known
2.	gouge	_____	b.	to scoop; to make a groove, hole, or indentation; to cut or force something out roughly or brutally
3.	barren	_____	c.	empty, bleak, and lifeless; (of land) too poor to produce substantial vegetation
4.	liberty	_____	d.	1. to drive back an attack or an enemy by force; 2. to cause someone to feel intense distaste and aversion
5.	repulse	_____	e.	1. the state of being free within society; the state of not being incarcerated or enslaved; 2. the power to act as one pleases

Sentences: Try to use the words above in a sentence below. Remember that a word ending may be changed or its figure of speech slightly altered.

6.   Lilly was _____ when her boyfriend threw up all over her new dress.

7.   Many Americans cherish the fact that they have the _____ of free speech and can thus voice themselves without concern.

8.   I hope the lady behind the counter _____ out a huge scoop of chocolate ice cream for me when I order.

9.   Polly couldn't help herself and thus _____ to the media that her sister was dating a prince.

10.   Much to the contrary of stereotypes, not all deserts are _____: some are sprawling with vegetation and animal life.

Lesson 22

PROHIBITION CULTURE

In the **era** known as Prohibition (1920-33), it was easy for a wealthy criminal to make money. Because the manufacture, transportation, and sale of alcohol was forbidden in the United States during this time, a crime boss could pay a **henchman** to smuggle liquor across the border from Canada. Activities of this sort had a **profound** effect on cities near the American border, thus creating a culture of illegal bootlegging. Yet the era quickly drew to a close as Americans strengthened their **stance** against prohibition. Though promoting drinking was hardly **exemplary**, the American government concluded that it was better to allow the sale of alcohol than to contend with an increase in gang fighting and illegal drinking joints (called *speakeasies*) than to try and enforce a complete nationwide ban on alcohol.

<table>
<tr><th>NEW WORDS</th></tr>
</table>

stance
stans

profound
prəˈfound, prō-

henchman
ˈhenCHmən

exemplary
igˈzemplərē

era
ˈi(ə)rə, ˈerə

Definitions: Try matching the words in the list with the appropriate definitions. If you are stuck, check the glossary in the back of the book or the passage at the top of the page.

1.	stance	_____	a.	1. serving as a desirable model; representing the best of its kind; 2. (in terms of punishment) serving as a warning or deterrent
2.	profound	_____	b.	1. (of a state, quality, or emotion) very great or intense; 2. (concerning a statement or person) having or showing great knowledge or insight
3.	henchman	_____	c.	a faithful supporter, especially one inclined to engage in unethical behavior by way of practice
4.	exemplary	_____	d.	1. the attitude of a person or organization toward something; 2. the way in which someone stands; posture
5.	era	_____	e.	a long and distinct period of history with a particular feature or characteristic

Sentences: Try to use the words above in a sentence below. Remember that a word ending may be changed or its figure of speech slightly altered.

6. We no longer live in a(n) _____ where people need to deliver mail on horseback.

7. One of Guido's _____ helped the criminals rob the bank.

8. Rather than being noncommittal, it is best to take a _____ in politics and fight for causes one believes in.

9. The Internet has had a(n) _____ impact on the way citizens communicate, learn, and transact their business.

10. Malik is a(n) _____ student: he always has his homework completed and receives excellent grades.

NEW WORDS

hygiene
ˈhī jēn

specter
ˈspektər

official
əˈfiSHəl

revelation
ˌrevəˈlāSHən

veto
ˈvētō

Lesson 23

THE CORRUPTED POLITICIAN

The **hygiene** levels observed in the neighborhood were despicable, and the **specter** of disease and famine hung over the dilapidated streets. A need for urgent measures was apparent, especially after the **revelation** that a number of children had died from malnutrition and sickness in the past month. The **official** record showed that some policies had been proposed to improve the conditions of the neighborhood; however, it became clear that the new mayor had used his power of **veto** to reject the proposed bills.

Definitions: Try matching the words in the list with the appropriate definitions. If you are stuck, check the glossary in the back of the book or the passage at the top of the page.

1.	hygiene	_____	a.	a constitutional right to reject a decision or a proposal made by a law-making body
2.	specter	_____	b.	a ghost
3.	official	_____	c.	conditions or practices conducive to maintaining health and preventing disease, especially through cleanliness
4.	revelation	_____	d.	a surprising and previously unknown fact, typically made or revealed in a dramatic way
5.	veto	_____	e.	(adj.) relating to an authority or body and its duties, actions, or responsibilities; (n.) a person holding public office and having official duties

Sentences: Try to use the words above in a sentence below. Remember that a word ending may be changed or its figure of speech slightly altered.

6.   Countries on the United Nations Security Council can _____ certain legislative acts.

7.   Yolanda broke up with her boyfriend because of his bad _____: she could no longer tolerate being near him for another minute without him showering.

8.   Walking through the spooky house, I was convinced that there was a(n) _____ haunting the corridor.

9.   Even though it looks like the Republican Party has won the election, television networks have yet to make a(n) _____ announcement of a party victory.

10.   It was a(n) _____ to Winona that she was adopted, for she thought that the individuals she had grown up with were her biological family.

Lesson 24

A TROUBLESOME TENANT

Aaqil regretted renting his friend Alex the upstairs floor of his house. Unemployed and irresponsible, Alex was not **willing** to pay the rent on time, and had put off doing so for four months. By **decree**, Aaqil had the right to **evict** Alex from his house. However, he still hesitated to take action. Knowing that Aaqil was softhearted, Alex often made empty promises that he would pay up soon, bribed Aaqil with **delectable** meals, and made **melodramatic** claims about true friendship.

NEW WORDS

evict
iˈvikt

melodramatic
ˌmelədrəˈmatik

delectable
diˈlektəbəl

decree
diˈkrē

willing
ˈwiliNG

Definitions: Try matching the words in the list with the appropriate definitions. If you are stuck, check the glossary in the back of the book or the passage at the top of the page.

1.   evict   _____   a.   to expel someone from a property with the assistance of the law
2.   melodramatic _____   b.   delicious; tasty
3.   delectable   _____   c.   ready, eager, or prepared to do something
4.   decree   _____   d.   overly emotional or dramatic
5.   willing   _____   e.   an official order issued by a ruler or legal authority

Sentences: Try to use the words above in a sentence below. Remember that a word ending may be changed or its figure of speech slightly altered.

6.   The korma dishes at the new Indian restaurant are _____.
7.   Having a friend who is _____ can be very emotionally taxing: dealing with myriad ups and downs can be very draining.
8.   The king issued a _____ that all subjects must wear pink floppy hats on Thursdays.
9.   Victor finally took action to _____ his tenant after the latter did not pay rent for three months.
10.   Unfortunately my parents are not _____ to pay for me to take a trip to Japan and learn about Kyoto's history.

NEW WORDS

chronic
ˈkränik

tangible
ˈtanjəbəl

contemporary
kənˈtempəˌrerē

retaliation
riˌtalēˈāSHən

medley
ˈmedlē

Lesson 25

THE BEGINNING OF THE END

As he began complaining of **chronic** fatigue due to work stress, his lack of interest in family matters became more and more **tangible**. He often would spend the evenings by himself listening to some weird jazz musician who sounded like a drunken **contemporary** of the swing musician Glenn Miller (1904-44). In **retaliation**, his wife stopped speaking to him almost entirely. She felt a **medley** of contradictory emotions: she still loved him, yet a certain hostility towards him began to creep into her heart.

Definitions: Try matching the words in the list with the appropriate definitions. If you are stuck, check the glossary in the back of the book or the passage at the top of the page.

1. chronic _____ a. the action of returning an attack; a counterattack
2. tangible _____ b. a varied mixture of people or things; a mixture
3. contemporary _____ c. 1. perceptible by touch; 2. clear and definite, real
4. retaliation _____ d. (adj.) 1. living or occurring at the same time; 2. belonging or occurring in the present; (n.) 1. a person or living thing existing at the same time as another; 2. a person of roughly the same age as another
5. medley _____ e. persisting for a long time or constantly recurring

Sentences: Try to use the words above in a sentence below. Remember that a word ending may be changed or its figure of speech slightly altered.

6. Tonight's symphony will contain a _____ of music from various early modern European maestros.

7. Johnny destroyed his brother's computer as _____ for the latter destroying the former's cell phone.

8. Ideas and concepts alone are not _____: only when they are developed or used for a practical end can one touch or hold the results.

9. The German mathematician Johannes Kepler (1571-1630) was a(n) _____ of the Danish astronomer Tycho Brahe (1546-1601); in fact, both men knew each other and briefly worked together in Prague.

10. Gambling has been a(n) _____ problem for Jerry, who has squandered his life savings playing poker over the years.

Lesson 26

THE MOMENT OF TRUTH

When the **soothsayer** predicted that Jack's wife would die from her heart disease, Jack simply could not react in a **rational** manner. He began to scream, to stomp his feet, and to **vent** his frustration. It became clear that the calm appearance that he possessed was a **camouflage** that hid his insecurities. To always seem happy and in control had been a major **objective** in Jack's life; however, on hearing the dismal predictions about his ill wife, he simply broke down.

NEW WORDS

vent
vent

soothsayer
ˈso͞oTHˌsāər

rational
ˈraSHənl, ˈraSHnəl

camouflage
ˈkaməˌfläZH, -ˌfläj

objective
əbˈjektiv

Definitions: Try matching the words in the list with the appropriate definitions. If you are stuck, check the glossary in the back of the book or the passage at the top of the page.

1.	vent	__________	a.	(adj.) not influenced by personal feelings; (n.) a thing aimed at or sought; a goal
2.	soothsayer	__________	b.	based on accordance with reason or logic
3.	rational	__________	c.	(n.) the disguising of people (especially military personnel), equipment, and installations by covering them to make them blend in with natural surroundings; material used for such disguise; an animal's covering that lets it blend in with natural surroundings; (v.) to hide or disguise the presence of a person, animal, or object; to conceal the existence of something undesirable
4.	camouflage	__________	d.	a person supposedly able to see the future
5.	objective	__________	e.	to give free expression to a strong emotion

Sentences: Try to use the words above in a sentence below. Remember that a word ending may be changed or its figure of speech slightly altered.

6. It is ____________________ to logically consider all of the successes and drawbacks before making a major life decision.
7. Chameleons are able to change color and thus ____________________ themselves in local surroundings to avoid being preyed upon.
8. Marion ____________________ her anger at Jake when she realized that he had lost his wedding ring.
9. The ____________________ of soccer is to score as many goals as possible while preventing the opposing team from doing so.
10. In many Asian cultures, it is customary to visit a(n) ____________________ to seek advice before embarking on a business venture.

NEW WORDS

plight
plīt

opulent
ˈäpyələnt

wound
wo͞ond

wreak
rēk

imply
imˈplī

Lesson 27

THE LOSS OF FAMILY PROPERTY

A businessman found himself in a sorry **plight**. The unstable market had begun to **wreak** havoc in his industry and he was losing his money and assets fast. Potential bankruptcy would **imply** that he could lose his **opulent** seaside villa. The subject of the villa became an open **wound** for the businessman: he could not bear the thought of losing the luxurious property, which had belonged to his family for nearly three centuries.

Definitions: Try matching the words in the list with the appropriate definitions. If you are stuck, check the glossary in the back of the book or the passage at the top of the page.

1.	plight	_____	a.	to inflict a large amount of harm or damage
2.	opulent	_____	b.	a difficult, dangerous, or unfortunate situation
3.	wound	_____	c.	to strongly suggest the truth, existence, or logical consequence of something
4.	wreak	_____	d.	ostentatiously rich and luxurious; extremely lavish
5.	imply	_____	e.	(n.) an injury to living tissue caused by a cut, blow, or other impact; (v.) to inflict an injury on someone

Sentences: Try to use the words above in a sentence below. Remember that a word ending may be changed or its figure of speech slightly altered.

6.   Timothy was _____ when his brother accidentally shot him with a BB gun.

7.   Though Katharine did not announce her departure, she _____ that such a decision was imminent when she delegated most of her responsibilities to coworkers.

8.   Many people are awed by the _____ décor in the palace of the Sultan of Brunei.

9.   The _____ of the coal workers was illuminated by the magazine, which published graphic pictures of their poor working conditions.

10.   Flooding near the coastline has _____ havoc on the local inhabitants.

Lesson 28

LIKE FATHER, LIKE DAUGHTER

The old man, who was now dying, had been a passionate **advocate** of human rights. Prior to his death, his daughter hired someone to **engrave** some of her father's most famous statements on his tombstone. She deeply respected her father and tried to imitate his stage presence whenever she spoke in front of an audience. She would even **mimic** his facial expressions and **swivel** her eyes in various directions the way her father had done before audiences. Losing him was an **ordeal** for her and she tried to be reminded of him in as many ways as possible.

NEW WORDS

engrave
enˈgrāv

advocate
ˈadvəkit (n.); -ˌkāt (v.)

swivel
ˈswivəl

mimic
ˈmimik

ordeal
ôrˈdēl

Definitions: Try matching the words in the list with the appropriate definitions. If you are stuck, check the glossary in the back of the book or the passage at the top of the page.

1.	engrave	_____	a.	to imitate someone's actions or words, typically with an attempt to ridicule
2.	advocate	_____	b.	a painful or horrific experience, often one that is protracted
3.	swivel	_____	c.	to cut or carve a text or design on the surface of a hard object
4.	mimic	_____	d.	(n.) a person who publicly supports or recommends a particular cause or policy; 2. a person who pleads on someone else's behalf; (v.) to publicly recommend or support
5.	ordeal	_____	e.	(n.) a coupling between two parts that enables one to revolve about the other; (v.) to turn about a point or axis on a coupling between two parts that enables one to revolve about the other

Sentences: Try to use the words above in a sentence below. Remember that a word ending may be changed or its figure of speech slightly altered.

6. Sally had the name of her favorite pet _____ on a locket, which contained a picture of her and her dog.

7. Most attorneys are hired to act as a(n) _____ on behalf of their clients.

8. Often apes _____ the behavior of their peers to learn social norms.

9. It was quite a(n) _____ to drive fifty miles in a blizzard.

10. Office chairs that _____ are much more relaxing to work in than simple stationary ones.

NEW WORDS

neophyte
ˈnēəˌfīt

daft
daft

divergent
diˈvərjənt, dī-

exonerate
igˈzänəˌrāt

empathy
ˈempəTHē

The two executive directors – one male and one female – of the multinational company have **divergent** policies regarding **neophyte** mishaps on the job. Generally it is always considered unfortunate when new, inexperienced employees miss the mark on specific tasks. However, the way that management addresses these mistakes differs along gender lines. While the male director shows great **empathy** and feels inclined to **exonerate** junior employees who make random mistakes, the female director shows only impatience before **daft** performance that embarrasses the company before its clients.

Definitions: Try matching the word in the box with the appropriate definition. If you are stuck, check the glossary in the back of the book or the passage at the top of the page.

1.   neophyte _____
2.   daft _____
3.   divergent _____
4.   exonerate _____
5.   empathy _____

a.   to absolve someone from blame for a wrongdoing
b.   a person who is new to a subject, skill, or belief
c.   silly; foolish
d.   tending to be different or to develop in different directions
e.   the ability to understand and share the feelings of another

Sentences: Try to use the words above in a sentence below. Remember that a word ending may be changed or its figure of speech slightly altered.

6.   Robert is a(n) _____ at golf: he has neither advanced skill nor expertise to beat a pro at a round of the game.

7.   Abbot was so _____ as to ask an obese, non-pregnant woman when her baby was due.

8.   New evidence presented to the police will help _____ Connie from being charged with murder.

9.   People who lack _____ for others are often construed as callous and narcissistic.

10. Jodi and Molly may be twins, but they took _____ life paths: one is a successful entrepreneur and the other is a waif.

Lesson 30

A MATTER OF CHARACTER

His **judicious** use of money even in more affluent times was one of the qualities she found attractive in her husband. They would order cheap Chinese food on big holidays. Going to **matinee** shows to save some money was another **idiosyncrasy** in his character. Most women would not see much **charisma** in a man who was so tight when it came to finances; however, she had always preferred **durable** and stable things, and she found Stephen's ways appealing.

Definitions: Try matching the words in the list with the appropriate definitions. If you are stuck, check the glossary in the back of the book or the passage at the top of the page.

1.	judicious _____	a.	having done or showing good judgment or sense
2.	idiosyncrasy _____	b.	a mode of behavior or way of thought peculiar to an individual; a distinctive characteristic peculiar to a person or thing
3.	matinee _____	c.	a daytime theater performance or movie showing
4.	charisma _____	d.	compelling attractiveness or charm that can inspire others
5.	durable _____	e.	able to withstand wear, pressure, or damage

Sentences: Try to use the words above in a sentence below. Remember that a word ending may be changed or its figure of speech slightly altered.

6.   New watches are more _____ than ones from a century ago: they can withstand getting wet or being dropped and stillb operate.

7.   Pundits believe that part of the reason Hillary was not elected is because she lacked the _____ to excite voters.

8.   It is _____ to consider all of the ramifications and minutiae of a business contract before signing it.

9.   One of Mai-Linh's _____ is that she talked to her stuffed animal raccoons every day.

10.   I prefer going to a _____ because evening cinema tickets are more expensive.

Word Search

Lessons 21-30

```
R  I  E  G  A  L  F  U  O  M  A  C  L
E  I  D  T  A  N  G  I  B  L  E  Y  L
V  E  M  I  L  A  N  O  I  T  A  R  Q
E  B  T  P  O  B  E  N  G  D  A  F  T
L  V  T  A  L  S  Y  L  V  O  D  T  H
A  D  A  K  R  Y  Y  O  B  S  U  E  N
T  E  V  R  E  E  C  N  T  A  N  G  H
I  C  S  L  G  A  N  A  C  C  R  Y  E
O  R  D  L  T  N  N  O  H  R  G  U  E
N  E  N  E  U  C  E  M  X  I  A  V  D
M  E  U  Q  E  P  A  R  E  E  I  S  B
Z  T  O  Y  N  N  E  N  Y  C  Y  Y  Y
R  B  W  K  Y  B  E  R  T  K  D  T  N
```

1 (v.) to scoop; to make a groove, hole, or indentation; to cut or force something out roughly or brutally
2 (v.) 1. to drive back an attack or an enemy by force; 2. to cause someone to feel intense distaste and aversion
3 (n.) 1. the attitude of a person or organization toward something; 2. the way in which someone stands; posture
4 (n.) a faithful supporter, especially one inclined to engage in unethical behavior by way of practice
5 (n.) conditions or practices conducive to maintaining health and preventing disease, especially through cleanliness
6 (n.) a surprising and previously unknown fact, typically made or revealed in a dramatic way
7 (v.) to expel someone from a property with the assistance of the law
8 (n.) an official order issued by a ruler or legal authority
9 (adj.) 1. perceptible by touch; 2. clear and definite, real
10 (n.) a varied mixture of people or things; a mixture
11 (adj.) based on accordance with reason or logic

12 (n.) the disguising of people (especially military personnel), equipment, and installations by covering them to make them blend in with natural surroundings; material used for such disguise; an animal's covering that lets it blend in with natural surroundings; (v.) to hide or disguise the presence of
13 (n.) an injury to living tissue caused by a cut, blow, or other impact; (v.) to inflict an injury on someone
14 (v.) to strongly suggest the truth, existence, or logical consequence of something
15 (v.) to cut or carve a text or design on the surface of a hard object
16 (n.) a person who publicly supports or recommends a particular cause or policy; 2. a person who pleads on someone else's behalf; (v.) to publicly recommend or support
17 (adj.) silly; foolish
18 (v.) to absolve someone from blame for a wrongdoing
19 (n.) a mode of behavior or way of thought peculiar to an individual; a distinctive characteristic peculiar to a person or thing
20 (adj.) able to withstand wear, pressure, or damage

Vocabulary Review
Lessons 21-30

Directions: Match each word with its best approximate definition. Note that definitions are not necessarily repeated verbatim from the lesson exercises.

1.	divulge	_____	a.	a beginner; a novice
2.	barren	_____	b.	to make known private or sensitive information
3.	profound	_____	c.	a dangerous, unfortunate, or difficult situation
4.	era	_____	d.	a daytime movie showing or theater performance
5.	specter	_____	e.	to reject; a constitutional right to reject a proposal or decision made by a legally authorized body
6.	veto	_____	f.	having, showing, or done with good judgment or sense
7.	melodramatic	_____	g.	desolate; empty; lacking signs of life
8.	delectable	_____	h.	tasty
9.	chronic	_____	i.	the action of harming someone in response to being harmed
10.	retaliation	_____	j.	to imitate another, typically with the intention to ridicule
11.	vent	_____	k.	a long, distinct period of history with a distinct feature or characteristic
12.	soothsayer	_____	l.	to cause or inflict a large amount of harm or damage
13.	plight	_____	m.	a ghost
14.	wreak	_____	n.	the ability to understand and share the feelings of another
15.	mimic	_____	o.	concerning a state, quality, or emotion that is very great or intense
16.	ordeal	_____	p.	to give free expression to a strong emotion
17.	neophyte	_____	q.	persisting for a long time or constantly recurring
18.	empathy	_____	r.	a painful, difficult, or horrific experience
19.	judicious	_____	s.	a person presumably able to see the future
20.	matinee	_____	t.	emotionally or sensationally exaggerated

Word Roots: Unit 3

ROOTS AND THEIR MEANINGS

phil:	love of	**intra:**	within, inside
pot:	power, ability	**culp:**	blame
omni:	all, every	**anthr/andr:**	man, mankind

Here are a few examples of some words that use the above roots:

phil<u></u>osophy:	the study of the nature of knowledge, reality, or existence
<u>pot</u>ent:	having great power, influence, or effect
<u>intra</u>mural:	situated or taking place within the walls of a building or within a single educational institution or community
<u>omnisci</u>ent:	knowing everything
<u>culp</u>rit:	a person who is responsible for a crime
<u>anthr</u>opology:	the study of humankind, its existence, its evolution, and its development

Now try to fill in the table below by finding the appropriate root(s) and interpreting the meaning of each word:

Word	Root(s)	Guessed Meaning	Actual Meaning
philanthropy			
omnipotent			
philology			
culpable			
anthropomorphic			
excrete			
android			
intravenous			
exculpate			
potentate			

Lesson 31

RIGHTING THE WRONGS OF THE PAST

James suddenly felt a **qualm** about the success of his business deal. He knew that his clients' interests were bound to **intersect** with his; however, he was also aware that the previous company owner had treated the same clients poorly. James became worried that the clients may not want to leave the past without any **redress**. Nevertheless, the business deal was very important to James and he decided to use his skills of **perseverance** and negotiation to see it through. He was going to **uphold** his initial position, regardless of what happened.

NEW WORDS

perseverance
ˌpərsəˈvi(ə)rəns

intersect
ˌintərˈsekt

uphold
ˌəpˈhōld

redress
kənˈsensəs

qualm
kwä(l)m, kwô(l)m

Definitions: Try matching the words in the list with the appropriate definitions. If you are stuck, check the glossary in the back of the book or the passage at the top of the page.

1.	perseverance _____	a.	(n.) a remedy or compensation for a wrong or grievance; (v.) to remedy or set right an undesirable situation
2.	intersect _____	b.	to divide something by passing or lying across it
3.	uphold _____	c.	steadfastness in doing something despite difficulty or delay in achieving success
4.	redress _____	d.	to confirm or support something that has happened; to maintain a custom or practice
5.	qualm _____	e.	an uneasy feeling of doubt, worry, or fear, especially about one's own conduct; a misgiving

Sentences: Try to use the words above in a sentence below. Remember that a word ending may be changed or its figure of speech slightly altered.

6. Doug did not know how to _____ the wrong that had happened when he ignored his wife, who begged him for help in an emergency.

7. Two parallel lines never _____.

8. I am impressed by Melinda's _____: in spite of losing her job and family, she has created a new career and vast support network.

9. It is hard for even the most self-assured people not to have _____ about some of their past behaviors.

10. The purpose of a sheriff is to _____ the law in any cases where it is challenged or obstructed.

NEW WORDS

limber
ˈlimbər

inadvertent
ˌinədˈvərtnt

gape
gāp

peculiar
pəˈkyoōlyər

negotiation
nəˌgōSHēˈāSHən

Harry's **negotiation** with the obese Chinese businessmen went sour after he made several **inadvertent** remarks about how corpulent people were lazy. As Harry denigrated overweight individuals, onlookers watched the **gape** in the Chinese businessman's mouth grow. Harry seemed to believe that only under **peculiar** circumstances could a heavy person be successful at a job. Furthermore, Harry equated career flexibility with physical flexibility: in his mind, only **limber** individuals were versatile enough to smoothly transition between careers. Unfortunately, only after the Chinese businessman abruptly got up and walked away did Harry realize that he was insulting and tactless in his remarks.

Definitions: Try matching the words in the list with the appropriate definitions. If you are stuck, check the glossary in the back of the book or the passage at the top of the page.

1.	limber	_____	a.	discussion aimed at reaching an agreement	
2.	inadvertent	_____	b.	to stare with one's mouth open wide, typically in amazement or wonder; to become wide or open	
3.	gape	_____	c.	not resulting from or achieved through deliberate planning	
4.	peculiar	_____	d.	1. strange or odd; unusual; 2. belonging exclusively to	
5.	negotiation	_____	e.	lithe; supple	

Sentences: Try to use the words above in a sentence below. Remember that a word ending may be changed or its figure of speech slightly altered.

6.   One of Myrna's _____ habits is that she always eats dessert before she eats a meal.

7.   Kel sat with his mouth _____ open after hearing that his parents had decided to get a divorce.

8.   Two countries often enter _____ to discuss terms of a bilateral trade agreement.

9.   Ian _____ tripped and stumbled down the steps, thus injuring his leg.

10.   Most gymnasts must have _____ bodies in order to be competitive.

Lesson 33

THE GAMING GENERATION

Martin was **hesitant** to allow his son to play video games because he was convinced that gaming had a **pernicious** effect on young children. He wanted his son to experience **gratification** from doing chores at home rather than only from pleasurable activities. However, the young boy could not escape the **fate** of his generation. He began to play video games at his friends' houses and became addicted to them: they provided such sheer **bliss** that he completely forgot his father's words.

NEW WORDS

bliss
blis

pernicious
pərˈniSHəs

fate
fāt

gratification
ˌgratəfiˈkāSHən

hesitant
ˈhezitənt

Definitions: Try matching the words in the list with the appropriate definitions. If you are stuck, check the glossary in the back of the book or the passage at the top of the page.

1.	bliss	_____	a.	perfect happiness; great joy
2.	pernicious	_____	b.	tentative, unsure, or slow in acting or speaking
3.	fate	_____	c.	pleasure, typically when attained from the satisfaction of a desire
4.	gratification	_____	d.	the development of events beyond a person's control, regarded as determined by a supernatural power
5.	hesitant	_____	e.	having a harmful effect, especially in a harmful or subtle way

Sentences: Try to use the words above in a sentence below. Remember that a word ending may be changed or its figure of speech slightly altered.

6.   Jonah was in a state of _____ when he found the long lost teddy bear from his childhood years after having supposed it had been indefinitely lost.

7.   Often two people who are enemies will say _____ things about each other.

8.   There is not much _____ in helping people who do not reciprocate or express their thanks for your efforts.

9.   The _____ of the passengers on the airliner was sealed as the plane's engines malfunctioned and it crashed into the ocean.

10.   Michael was _____ to take a job offer in Hong Kong because he was not sure if he could trust his potential new supervisor.

NEW WORDS

stature
ˈstaCHər

maneuver
məˈnoōvər

dexterity
dekˈsteritē

lethargic
ləˈTHärjik

accommodate
əˈkäməˌdāt

Lesson 34

LIFE AFTER WORK

Back in the day, Adam had been a man of international **stature** in the business world. Selling the biggest company in his country to foreign investors was an extremely risky yet successful **maneuver**. Adam was known for his verbal **dexterity** and ability to persuade others. He always found a way to **accommodate** even the most demanding clients. After retirement, however, Adam became a shadow of himself. He remained in bed all day, **lethargic** and apathetic, as if nothing in the world interested him any longer.

Definitions: Try matching the words in the list with the appropriate definitions. If you are stuck, check the glossary in the back of the book or the passage at the top of the page.

1.	stature	_____	a.	sluggish, apathetic
2.	maneuver	_____	b.	(n.) a movement or series of moves that requires skill and care; 2. a carefully planned scheme or action; (v.) 1. to move skillfully or carefully; 2. to carefully guide or manipulate something or someone to achieve an end
3.	dexterity	_____	c.	1. to provide lodging or sufficient space for; 2.to fit in with the wishes or needs of
4.	lethargic	_____	d.	1. a person's natural height; 2.importance or reputation gained by ability or achievement
5.	accommodate	_____	e.	skill at performing tasks, especially with the hands

Sentences: Try to use the words above in a sentence below. Remember that a word ending may be changed or its figure of speech slightly altered.

6.   Bill epitomized a(n) _____ person: he sat on the couch all day eating potato chips instead of doing something energizing and productive.

7.   In general, dwarves are beings that have a very short or small _____.

8.   It is difficult to _____ one's car through traffic during rush hour in Oakland.

9.   Most airlines can _____ special dietary needs of travelers who notify them in advance of their requirements and/or restrictions.

10.   In order to be an effective magician, one must possess great _____, especially with his or her hands.

Lesson 35

THE IMPORTANCE OF BEING FRIENDLY

The prisoner was able to **construe** from his inmates' facial expressions that he was not welcome at their table. His peers often would **expel** him from communal activities, hoping that their actions would **goad** him into becoming more socially aggressive. However, the prisoner found that his natural shyness was a powerful **barrier** to generating any closer contact. Even the guards found him passive. The warden, however, was more **lenient** with the prisoner in his words: perhaps the warden just felt sorry for him.

NEW WORDS

construe
kən'stroō

goad
gōd

expel
ik'spel

barrier
'barēər

lenient
'lēnēənt, 'lēnyənt

Definitions: Try matching the words in the list with the appropriate definitions. If you are stuck, check the glossary in the back of the book or the passage at the top of the page.

1.	construe	_____	a.	(of punishment or a person in authority) tending to be permissive, merciful or tolerant
2.	goad	_____	b.	to interpret a word or action in a particular way
3.	expel	_____	c.	to provoke or annoy someone so as to stimulate some action or reaction
4.	barrier	_____	d.	an object that prevents movement or access
5.	lenient	_____	e.	to deprive someone membership or involvement in a school or organization; to force someone to leave a place

Sentences: Try to use the words above in a sentence below. Remember that a word ending may be changed or its figure of speech slightly altered.

6. Frida's mom _____ her daughter's excitement about going to the theme park with friends as a sign of her love for rollercoasters, not a sign of thrill to escape the family.

7. During the years 1961-1989, the Berlin Wall served as a(n) _____ that divided East and West Germany into respective capitalist and communist parts.

8. Sanford was _____ from school after he tried to punch his principal in the face.

9. If parents are too _____ with rules for their children, such children may not learn how to discipline themselves in order to be successful.

10. Ariel's friends tried to _____ her into making fun of the old man, but Ariel obstinately refused.

NEW WORDS

apathy
'apəTHē

realize
'rē(ə)ˌlīz

diverse
diˈvərs, dī-

vehement
'vēəmənt

virtuous
'vərCHəwəs

Lindsey had been leading a quiet and **virtuous** life, with a clear **apathy** for social engagement. However, when her best friend Jim was lynched for his outspoken stance on Jim Crow laws, Lindsey began to **realize** that she needed to take action and became a strong advocate of civil rights. She gathered a **diverse** group of people who shared the same sentiments and led a **vehement** protest against racial segregation and abuse. Lindsey also founded an organization that offered assistance to African Americans who struggled financially.

Definitions: Try matching the words in the list with the appropriate definitions. If you are stuck, check the glossary in the back of the book or the passage at the top of the page.

1. apathy   _____   a.   lack of interest, enthusiasm, or concern
2. realize   _____   b.   showing a great deal of variety; very different
3. diverse   _____   c.   showing strong feeling, especially forceful, passionate, or intense
4. vehement   _____   d.   1. to become fully aware of something as fact; 2. to cause something desired or anticipated to happen; 3. to give actual or physical form to an idea or plan; 4. to make money or a profit from a transaction
5. virtuous   _____   e.   exhibiting high moral standards

Sentences: Try to use the words above in a sentence below. Remember that a word ending may be changed or its figure of speech slightly altered.

6. Sandra's mother was _____ about forbidding her daughter to go out late at night because it was unsafe.

7. It is not always easy to _____ when someone is covertly trying to manipulate you in a business deal.

8. Unlike many other countries, America contains a(n) _____ set of cultures and races within its borders.

9. Generally, honest and hard working people are seen to be _____ and to possess good character.

10. Lindsay was _____ about going to lunch with her girlfriends: she did not seem to care one way or another whether she saw them in the afternoon for a meal.

Lesson 37

TO SELL A VIDEO GAME

There was a **glut** of video games on the market. To make his game stand out, James sought to find an item that would **accompany** it, thus making the game more visible in stores. James also hoped to **reduce** the price of his video game by using less expensive packaging. A successful new video game, he thought, would **quell** the fears in his company that it could go bankrupt, and James's usually **garrulous** employees had become very reserved under such circumstances. James believed that launching his product would raise their spirits, and he was determined to have his colleagues help him find a way to sell his newest product.

NEW WORDS

glut
glət

garrulous
ˈgar(y)ələs

reduce
riˈd(y)o͞os

accompany
əˈkəmp(ə)nē

quell
kwel

Definitions: Try matching the words in the list with the appropriate definitions. If you are stuck, check the glossary in the back of the book or the passage at the top of the page.

1. glut _____
2. garrulous _____
3. reduce _____
4. accompany _____
5. quell _____

a. excessively talkative in a roundabout way, especially on trivial matters
b. an excessively abundant supply of something
c. to put an end to rebellion or disorder, usually by force
d. to make or become smaller in size, amount, or degree
e. to go somewhere with someone as a companion or escort; to be present or occur at the same time as something else; to provide something as a complement or addition to something else

Sentences: Try to use the words above in a sentence below. Remember that a word ending may be changed or its figure of speech slightly altered.

6. There is a(n) _____ of golf balls in the country club pro shop; the store is almost completely filled with them!
7. The police did little to _____ the raging protests downtown: people kept demonstrating throughout the night.
8. This cake is too sweet! Next time you make it you should _____ the amount of sugar you use in the batter.
9. It is standard for American presidents to be _____ by secret service members when they go out of the White House.
10. Unlike Todd, who is by nature reticent, Doris is rather _____.

NEW WORDS

settle
ˈsetl

foundation
founˈdāSHən

void
void

inscribe
inˈskrīb

terminate
ˈtərməˌnāt

Lesson 38

MEMORIES AND NEW BEGINNINGS

After a three-week voyage, the couple decided to **terminate** their journey and **settle** in a small mountainous village. They wanted to build a new **foundation** for their lives there, unencumbered by the past. The death of their child had left a huge **void** in their lives, but they knew they had to start their lives over. The man asked a local stone mason to **inscribe** the name of the child over a mantelpiece for them. They hoped that seeing the child's name everyday would bring them some comfort and the necessary strength to move on.

Definitions: Try matching the words in the list with the appropriate definitions. If you are stuck, check the glossary in the back of the book or the passage at the top of the page.

1.	settle	_____	a.	1. to resolve or reach an agreement an argument or problem; 2. to adopt a more steady and secure lifestyle, usually with a job and a home; 3. to sit or come to rest in a comfortable position
2.	foundation	_____	b.	to bring to an end
3.	void	_____	c.	to write or carve words or symbols on something, especially as a permanent record
4.	inscribe	_____	d.	1. the lowest load-bearing part of a building, typically underground; 2. the underlying basis or principle for something; 3. an institution or organization with an endowment
5.	terminate	_____	e.	(adj.) 1. not valid or legally binding; 2. completely empty; (n.) a completely empty space; (v.) to declare that something is not valid or legally binding

Sentences: Try to use the words above in a sentence below. Remember that a word ending may be changed or its figure of speech slightly altered.

6.   By the age of forty, most people have decided to _____ with a spouse and have a home and children.

7.   The _____ of a healthy relationship is clear, honest communication.

8.   Companies unable to pay their full workforce must _____ employees.

9.   After my cat Chairman Meow died, I felt a(n) _____ in my life: there was no purring buddy to lift my spirits when I was lonely or down.

10.   Brandon _____ the name of his girlfriend on a bracelet and gave it to her as a birthday gift.

Lesson 39

EMERGENCY IN THE HOTEL

As John walked down the corridor, he saw an **obese** man lying on the floor. The man looked at him and whispered that John needed to go into the his room and get his medicine immediately. He was panting heavily and sweating profusely. John approached the stranger's room with **trepidation**. He felt that going through someone's personal things was a **breach** of privacy. In addition, he only had a **rudimentary** knowledge of the man's condition. At the same time, he knew that he needed to **lull** the man's anxiety until the paramedics came.

NEW WORDS

breach
brēCH

lull
ləl

obese
ōˈbēs

rudimentary
ˌro͞odəˈment(ə)rē

trepidation
ˌtrepiˈdāSHən

Definitions: Try matching the words in the list with the appropriate definitions. If you are stuck, check the glossary in the back of the book or the passage at the top of the page.

1.   breach   _____   a.   a feeling of fear or agitation about something that may happen

2.   lull   _____   b.   involving or limited to basic principles

3.   obese   _____   c.   (n.) a temporary interval of quiet or lack of activity; (v.) to calm or send to sleep typically with soothing sounds or movements

4.   rudimentary _____   d.   grossly fat or overweight

5.   trepidation _____   e.   (n.) 1. an act of breaking a law, agreement, or code of conduct; 2. a gap in a wall, barrier, or defense made by an army; (v.) to break a law, agreement, or code of conduct; 2. to make a gap in and break through a wall, barrier, or defense

Sentences: Try to use the words above in a sentence below. Remember that a word ending may be changed or its figure of speech slightly altered.

6.   When someone _____ another person's trust, the relationship between both people can be seriously jeopardized.

7.   Usually there is a _____ in tempestuous weather when one is in the eye of a hurricane.

8.   With much _____, the princess watched in fear as the knight tried to slay the dragon attacking her palace.

9.   Tommy is still struggling with _____ math skills: each week I try to ensure that he knows his multiplication tables.

10.   A person who weighs 500 pounds is certainly _____.

NEW WORDS

dilapidated
di'lapi͵dātid

ratify
'ratə͵fī

manufacture
͵manyə'fakCHər

presage
'presij, pri'sāj

truce
tro͞os

PICKING UP THE PIECES

The battle left remains of buildings and **dilapidated** houses everywhere. Following a **truce** between the two warring sides, representatives of both parties decided to **ratify** laws to reopen local factories. After much destruction, the factories needed to **manufacture** many new products so that life in the region could resume. It was clear that a spirit of economic resurgence had to **presage** decisions about the political future of the region.

Definitions: Try matching the words in the list with the appropriate definitions. If you are stuck, check the glossary in the back of the book or the passage at the top of the page.

1. dilapidated _____   a. to sign or give formal consent to a law, agreement, or treaty to render it valid

2. ratify _____   b. (n.) a sign or warning that something (typically bad) will happen; an omen or portent; (v.) (of an event) to be a sign that something (typically bad) will happen

3. manufacture _____   c. (n.) the making of articles on a large scale using machinery; (v.) 1. to make something on a large scale using machinery; 2. to invent or fabricate evidence or story

4. presage _____   d. a building or object in a state of disrepair or ruin as a result of age or neglect

5. truce _____   e. an agreement between enemies or opponents to stop fighting

Sentences: Try to use the words above in a sentence below. Remember that a word ending may be changed or its figure of speech slightly altered.

6. Jane's untimely death was _____ by a high fever and a loss of appetite.

7. If you do not take care of your home it will become _____ over time, thus requiring substantial renovation to maintain it.

8. Congress must _____ the bill before new rules can be put into action.

9. In the twentieth century, Detroit had many automotive plants where cars were _____.

10. After fighting for twenty years, the two countries called a _____ and ceased fighting.

Crossword Puzzle
Lessons 31-40

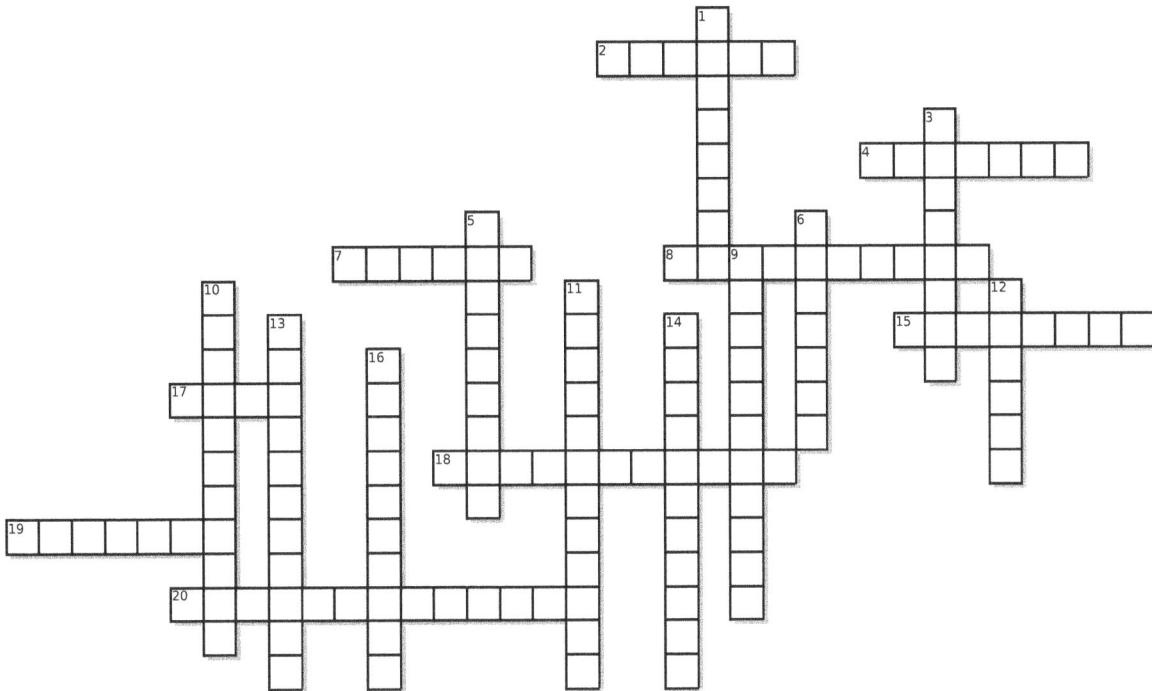

ACROSS

2 (v.) to confirm or support something that has happened; to maintain a custom or practice
4 (n.) 1. a person's natural height; 2.importance or reputation gained by ability or achievement
7 (v.) to make or become smaller in size, amount, or degree
8 (adj.) having a harmful effect, especially in a harmful or subtle way
15 (adj.) showing strong feeling, especially forceful, passionate, or intense
17 (n.) a temporary interval of quiet or lack of activity; (v.) to calm or send to sleep typically with soothing sounds or movements
18 (adj.) not resulting from or achieved through deliberate planning
19 (adj.) (of punishment or a person in authority) tending to be permissive, merciful or tolerant
20 (n.) pleasure, typically when attained from the satisfaction of a desire

DOWN

1 (v.) to interpret a word or action in a particular way
3 (n.) a movement or series of moves that requires skill and care; 2. a carefully planned scheme or action; (v.) 1. to move skillfully or carefully; 2. to carefully guide or manipulate something or someone to achieve an end
5 (v.) to go somewhere with someone as a companion or escort; to be present or occur at the same time as something else; to provide something as a complement or addition to something else
6 (adj.) showing a great deal of variety; very different
9 (adj.) involving or limited to basic principles
10 (n.) the making of articles on a large scale using machinery; (v.) 1. to make something on a large scale using machinery; 2. to invent or fabricate evidence or a story
11 (n.) steadfastness in doing something despite difficulty or delay in achieving success
12 (v.) 1. to resolve or reach an agreement an argument or problem; 2. to adopt a more steady and secure lifestyle, usually with a job and a home; 3. to sit or come to rest in a comfortable position
13 (adj.) a building or object in a state of disrepair or ruin as a result of age or neglect
14 (n.) discussion aimed at reaching an agreement
16 (n.) 1. the lowest load-bearing part of a building, typically underground; 2. the underlying basis or principle for something; 3. an institution or organization with an endowment

Vocabulary Review
Lessons 31-40

Directions: Match each word with its best approximate definition. Note that definitions are not necessarily repeated verbatim from the lesson exercises.

1.	intersect	_____	a.	strange, odd, or unusual
2.	qualm	_____	b.	exhibiting high moral standards
3.	limber	_____	c.	an excessively abundant supply of something
4.	peculiar	_____	d.	an uneasy feeling of doubt
5.	bliss	_____	e.	an agreement between enemies or opponents to stop fighting for a time
6.	hesitant	_____	f.	excessively talkative in a roundabout way
7.	dexterity	_____	g.	to write or carve words into something
8.	lethargic	_____	h.	unsure or tentative in acting or speaking
9.	goad	_____	i.	skill in performing tasks, especially with the hands
10.	barrier	_____	j.	great joy or perfect happiness
11.	apathy	_____	k.	an obstacle – literal or intangible – that prevents access or progress
12.	virtuous	_____	l.	feeling of fear that something bad may happen
13.	glut	_____	m.	concerning a body part that is lithe; supple
14.	garrulous	_____	n.	lack of interest, enthusiasm, or concern
15.	void	_____	o.	to divide something by passing or lying across it
16.	inscribe	_____	p.	to provoke or annoy someone with the hope that a reaction will be solicited
17.	obese	_____	q.	to give formal consent to a treaty, thus making it valid
18.	trepidation	_____	r.	grossly overweight
19.	ratify	_____	s.	sluggish and apathetic
20.	truce	_____	t.	an emptiness; not valid or legally binding

Word Roots: Unit 4

ROOTS AND THEIR MEANINGS

super:	over, beyond	**post:**	after
terr:	earth	**bel(l):**	war
amb:	walk	**trans:**	across
mis/mit:	to send	**fid:**	trust, faith

Here are a few examples of some words that use the above roots:

superhero:	a fictional icon who does good deeds and who possesses powers greater than what humans are capable of possessing
terracentric:	a model or system of the universe in which the Earth is at the center rather than the sun.
amble:	to walk in a casual, relaxed, slow pace
postdate:	to assign a later date than the actual one to a document or event
bellicose:	exhibiting aggression and willingness to fight
transcend:	to go beyond the range or limits of something
remit:	to send money in payment as form of a gift (one of many definitions of remit)
fidelity:	faithfulness to a person, belief, or cause by showing signs of support and/or loyalty

Now try to fill in the table below by finding the appropriate root(s) and interpreting the meaning of each word:

Word	Root(s)	Guessed Meaning	Actual Meaning
intermittent			
amble			
transnational			
belligerent			
fiduciary			
transmit			
subterranean			

posterior			
rebellion			
supercede			
terrain			
superconductor			
infidelity			
terrarium			
ambulatory			
missive			
transit			

Lesson 41

DISORDER IN THE CLASSROOM

The atmosphere in the classroom became **turbulent** when a few boys began fighting and screaming. It was an **uncanny** sight for the new teacher who gave them a **stern** look. The boys did not seem intimidated by the new teacher, who tried to **upbraid** the students for the classroom fight. Upon seeing that he could not solve the problem with his voice alone, the teacher realized that **superficial** measurements would not suffice; he needed to take the boys to the headmaster to solve the matter.

NEW WORDS

turbulent
ˈtərbyələnt

uncanny
ˌənˈkanē

stern
stərn

upbraid
ˌəpˈbrād

superficial
ˌsoōpərˈfiSHəl

Definitions: Try matching the words in the list with the appropriate definitions. If you are stuck, check the glossary in the back of the book or the passage at the top of the page.

1.	turbulent	_____	a.	strange or mysterious in an unsettling way
2.	uncanny	_____	b.	(adj.) describing a person who is serious and unrelenting, especially in matters of assertion of authority and exertion of discipline; strict and severe; (n.) the rearmost part of a ship or boat
3.	stern	_____	c.	existing or occurring on the surface; not thorough, deep, or complete; shallow
4.	upbraid	_____	d.	characterized by conflict, disorder, or confusion; liquid that moves violently and unsteadily
5.	superficial	_____	e.	to scold; to find fault with someone

Sentences: Try to use the words above in a sentence below. Remember that a word ending may be changed or its figure of speech slightly altered.

6. A flight can experience great _____ when an airplane flies through an air pocket.

7. Akisha _____ her sister when the latter forgot to attend the former's birthday party.

8. That woman on the train station bench bears a(n) _____ resemblance to the American actress, Emma Stone.

9. Luckily, Rodney's wound was only _____: beneath the surface of his skin, there was no deep damage to underlying muscles or tissue.

10. Unlike Max, who is lax, Vern is rather _____ in his dealings.

NEW WORDS

debris
də'brē, ˌdā-

intricate
'intrikit

meager
'mēgər

hypocrisy
hi'päkrisē

insurgent
in'sərjənt

Lesson 42

THE AFTERMATH

The recent bombing incident left the embassy buried in **debris** and killed many innocent civilians. The culprit, claiming to be fed up with the **hypocrisy** of the government in dealing with its foreign affairs, had devised an **intricate** bombing plan to take matters into his own hands. Since the damage of such a terrorist act was severe, this **insurgent** was sentenced to death. Worried that the current **meager** protection of governmental buildings could not withstand future attacks, the local government also tightened its security.

Definitions: Try matching the words in the list with the appropriate definitions. If you are stuck, check the glossary in the back of the book or the passage at the top of the page.

1.	debris	_____	a.	(adj.) rising in active revolt; (n.) a rebel or revolutionary
2.	intricate	_____	b.	lacking in quantity or quality
3.	meager	_____	c.	scattered fragments of something wrecked or destroyed
4.	hypocrisy	_____	d.	the practice of claiming to have certain moral standards or beliefs to which one's behavior does not conform
5.	insurgent	_____	e.	very complicated or detailed

Sentences: Try to use the words above in a sentence below. Remember that a word ending may be changed or its figure of speech slightly altered.

6.   After San Francisco's giant 1906 earthquake, _____ from crumbled buildings was found all across town.

7.   I was expecting a giant platter at Devon's dinner party, but instead was served only a(n) _____ three grains of rice!

8.   The design on the Persian carpet was _____ and contained images of many shapes in many colors.

9.   The _____ populace held a coup and deposed the king.

10.   Louisa sensed _____ when her parents demand she have a lucrative career after college; when she was young they had told her to follow her dreams regardless of income.

Lesson 43

BROTHERLY RELATIONS

Two brothers bought a copper tank as a **souvenir** from the history museum. The older brother, Tom, commanded his younger sibling to **burnish** the tank every day. The younger child, Tin, was **meek** and gentle and accepted the order – likely because he feared Tom's **pugnacious** nature. Moreover, Tom often would hurl hurtful **barbed** comments at his little brother, thus helping to motivate Tin's willing compliance.

Definitions: Try matching the words in the list with the appropriate definitions. If you are stuck, check the glossary in the back of the book or the passage at the top of the page.

1.	pugnacious	_____	a.	quiet, gentle, submissive; easily imposed upon
2.	souvenir	_____	b.	to polish
3.	barbed	_____	c.	eager to argue, quarrel, or fight
4.	burnish	_____	d.	a thing kept as a reminder of a person, place, or event
5.	meek	_____	e.	having sharp projections on an object so as to make extraction difficult; deliberately hurtful

Sentences: Try to use the words above in a sentence below. Remember that a word ending may be changed or its figure of speech slightly altered.

6. Robin is often _____ and enjoys picking fights with her coworkers.
7. Magnets, spoons, and figurines are among my favorite _____ to purchase when I travel to an exotic place.
8. Unlike Sean, who is tactful, Daryl's _____ comments have often offended other people.
9. Being a socialite is not a lifestyle for the _____: one is perpetually in the limelight and media in this role.
10. Eileen spent hours trying to _____ her resume so that it looked attractive to potential employers.

NEW WORDS

feral
ˈfi(ə)rəl, ˈferəl

quarantine
ˈkwôrənˌtēn

atrophy
ˈatrəfē

robust
rōˈbəst, ˈrōˌbəst

pliable
ˈplīəbəl

Mr. Ford's pet dog was put temporarily into **quarantine** after it had arrived in the new country. Such a policy was standard practice, as the nation needed to ensure that all pets entering its borders were **robust** and not **feral**. Luckily for Mr. Ford, his dog was healthy. Despite the long voyage, none of the dog's muscles had begun to **atrophy** and the dog was excited to jump about and fetch balls. It even enjoyed gnawing on a **pliable** rubber toy that stretched when pulled. The dog appeared to have completed its overseas voyage in good spirits, and Mr. Ford was happy to begin a new chapter of his life with his canine buddy.

Definitions: Try matching the words in the list with the appropriate definitions. If you are stuck, check the glossary in the back of the book or the passage at the top of the page.

1. feral _____
   a. (n.) a state, period, or place of isolation in which people or animals that have arrived from elsewhere or been exposed to infectious or contagious diseases have been placed; (v.) to impose isolation on a person or animal (typically one carrying a disease)

2. quarantine _____
   b. strong and healthy; vigorous

3. atrophy _____
   c. 1. for a body tissue to waste away, typically due to the degeneration of cells; 2. to gradually decline in effectiveness or vigor due to underuse or neglect

4. robust _____
   d. 1. easily bent; flexible; 2. easily influenced

5. pliable _____
   e. (usually of an animal) in a wild state, especially after escaping domesticity or captivity

Sentences: Try to use the words above in a sentence below. Remember that a word ending may be changed or its figure of speech slightly altered.

6. Residents in my town having contracted the deadly plague were _____ so that others would not be infected.

7. If one does not keep up with weight lifting, his or her muscles will _____ in time.

8. Unlike dogs, coyotes are _____ animals unsuited to dwell with humans.

9. The town's annual celebration was quite _____; it included a number of festivities ranging from fireworks to street art to two live concerts.

10. Unlike wood, which snaps and breaks under pressure, rubber is more _____ when outside forces act on it.

Lesson 45

THE SECRET SUPPORTER

After receiving no government funding for his research, Martin did not even have a **modicum** of hope to see his project materialize. However, by some strange **cosmic** circumstance, on the last day before the funding deadline, an **anonymous** donor decided to **contribute** a large amount of money to support Martin's project. It was nothing short of a miracle. Martin did not know whether it was a **random** coincidence that someone had seen his project at the last minute or whether some affluent person had been observing his work for a long time and finally decided to help.

NEW WORDS

modicum
ˈmädikəm, ˈmōd-

anonymous
əˈnänəməs

cosmic
ˈkäzmik

random
ˈrandəm

contribute
kənˈtribyo͞ot, -byət

Definitions: Try matching the words in the list with the appropriate definitions. If you are stuck, check the glossary in the back of the book or the passage at the top of the page.

1.	modicum _____	a.	of or relating to the universe or things beyond Earth
2.	anonymous _____	b.	to give (something, often money) in order to help achieve or provide something
3.	cosmic _____	c.	a small quantity of a particular thing, especially one that is valuable
4.	random _____	d.	(of a person) not identified by name, or of unknown name
5.	contribute _____	e.	made, done, or chosen without method or conscious thought

Sentences: Try to use the words above in a sentence below. Remember that a word ending may be changed or its figure of speech slightly altered.

6.   If scientists unearthed a new planet in our solar system, such a finding would challenge our notion of the _____ order.

7.   Drawing names out of a hat to win a prize is a very _____ way to select winners.

8.   Some people believe it is best to give _____ feedback rather than to furnish one's name next to criticism.

9.   Daniel was so selfish that he didn't even have a(n) _____ of concern about how his actions could impact others.

10.   Smoking, alcoholism, and lack of exercise all _____ to one appearing physically aged.

NEW WORDS

deter
di'tər

bounty
'bountē

drawback
'drô,bak

request
ri'kwest

predate
prē'dāt

Lesson 46

A CHANGE IN POLICY

The computer programming camp was well known for its quality, as its graduates typically received a **bounty** of job offers within one year of completing the program. Yet a major **drawback** of the camp that might **deter** some people from signing up was its exorbitant cost. To attract a more diverse pool of participants, the head of the camp decided to lower the price and offer scholarships for students from low-income backgrounds. Any student already registered for the upcoming camp whose payment might **predate** the adoption of this policy could still **request** a partial refund.

Definitions: Try matching the words in the list with the appropriate definitions. If you are stuck, check the glossary in the back of the book or the passage at the top of the page.

1.   deter   _____   a.   a feature that renders something less acceptable; a disadvantage or problem

2.   bounty   _____   b.   (n.) an act of asking politely or formally for something; (v.) to ask politely or formally for something

3.   drawback   _____   c.   to discourage someone from doing something, typically by instilling doubt or fear

4.   request   _____   d.   to exist or occur at a date earlier than something

5.   predate   _____   e.   1. generosity, liberality; abundance; 2. a monetary gift or reward given by a government, usually for killing or capturing a criminal

Sentences: Try to use the words above in a sentence below. Remember that a word ending may be changed or its figure of speech slightly altered.

6.   There is a(n) _____ of ten thousand dollars for anyone who can bring the outlaw to the sheriff, who will deliver justice.

7.   Little could _____ Tiffany's strong interest in quitting her job and moving to Barbados.

8.   Barbara made a(n) _____ to her boss for a week off so that she could attend her sister's wedding in Almaty.

9.   One of the _____ of living in Boston is that the winter climate can be unbearable for many people.

10.   Alphabetic language seems to _____ the birth of Christianity in world history.

69

Lesson 47

THE REVIVAL

The company business had fallen into a boring **routine** after feelings of complacency had managed to **invade** its leadership. Perhaps it was a sign of **mercy** to the CEO that a new and exciting client appeared out of nowhere and boosted the morale of the corporate management. Little by little, the company began to operate at full **blast** again after many months of stagnation. Within a year, there was a **stampede** of new applicants who were applying for jobs at the company and the business began to grow.

Definitions: Try matching the words in the list with the appropriate definitions. If you are stuck, check the glossary in the back of the book or the passage at the top of the page.

1.   routine   _____   a.   (n.) a sudden panicked rush of a number of horses, cattle, or other animals; (v.) (of horses, cattle, or other animals) to rush wildly in a sudden mass

2.   mercy   _____   b.   for an armed forces to enter a region and occupy it; to enter an area in large numbers; for a disease to spread into an organism or body part; to encroach or intrude on

3.   blast   _____   c.   compassion or forgiveness shown toward someone whom it is within one's power to punish or harm

4.   stampede   _____   d.   (adj.) performed as part of regular procedure; (n.) a sequence of actions regularly followed

5.   invade   _____   e.   (n.) 1. a destructive wave of compressed air spreading outward from an explosion; 2. a strong gust of wind or air; 3. a single loud noise emanating from a horn or other musical instrument; (v.) 1. to blow up or break apart something with explosives; 2. to make or cause to make a loud continuous musical or other noise

Sentences: Try to use the words above in a sentence below. Remember that a word ending may be changed or its figure of speech slightly altered.

6.   Lizzie ran to the curb as a(n) _____ of horses ran down the highway.

7.   Dave likes having a(n) _____ that he can follow to keep him on task.

8.   The despotic pharaoh showed no _____ for his subjects and forced many of them to travail in the punishing weather to build his pyramids.

9.   When I exited the casino, a(n) _____ of air flew in my face.

10.   The horror film is about aliens that _____ Earth and destroy humans.

NEW WORDS

taciturn
ˈtasiˌtərn

glint
glint

manifold
ˈmanəˌfōld

communicate
kəˈmyo͞onəˌkāt

salutation
ˌsalyəˈtāSHən

Lesson 48

THE MYSTERIOUS NEIGHBOR

The little boy greeted the old neighbor every morning but the man would only respond with a **taciturn** look at his **salutation**. It was obvious that the old man did not want to **communicate** with anyone, least of all with a little child. The boy had **manifold** interests every day so he would forget about the old man quickly. However, every time that he saw the old neighbor through the window, there was a **glint** of recognition and curiosity in his eyes.

Definitions: Try matching the words in the list with the appropriate definitions. If you are stuck, check the glossary in the back of the book or the passage at the top of the page.

1.	taciturn	_____	a.	to share or exchange information, news, or ideas
2.	glint	_____	b.	a gesture or utterance made as a greeting or acknowledgement of another's arrival or departure
3.	manifold	_____	c.	(n.) a small flash of light; (of one's eyes) a shine with a particular emotion; (v.) to give out or reflect small flashes of light
4.	communicate	_____	d.	a person who is reserved and uncommunicative in speech; saying little
5.	salutation	_____	e.	many and various

Sentences: Try to use the words above in a sentence below. Remember that a word ending may be changed or its figure of speech slightly altered.

6.   The reasons for my moving from Cleveland to Miami are _____: I prefer warm weather, there are more job opportunities in the latter location, and I have relatives there.

7.   Waving hello when one arrives is a common _____ in America and much of Europe.

8.   Even though Jay was depressed, I could still sense a(n) _____ of hope in his eyes that he could create a successful and profound future.

9.   It can be difficult for two people from different cultures to _____ effectively, as each person has different values and mores.

10.   The _____ librarian sat at her desk reading books and rarely spoke unless she was addressed.

Lesson 49

A SWEET REVENGE

The teenagers decided to **vandalize** the car of the richest boy in class. They were **deft** with their instruments and were able to open the car within seconds. The rich boy's **blatant** superiority had made them very angry. He would **jeer** at them and humiliate them in front of others because they were the poorest kids in school. This served as a strong **incentive** for the boys to damage the expensive car.

NEW WORDS

blatant
ˈblātnt

jeer
ji(ə)r

incentive
inˈsentiv

vandalize
ˈvandlˌīz

deft
deft

Definitions: Try matching the words in the list with the appropriate definitions. If you are stuck, check the glossary in the back of the book or the passage at the top of the page.

1.	blatant	_____	a.	a thing that motivates or encourages one to do something
2.	jeer	_____	b.	typically bad behavior done openly and unashamedly
3.	incentive	_____	c.	neatly skillful and quick in one's movements
4.	vandalize	_____	d.	(n.) a rude, mocking remark; (v.) to make rude and mocking comments, typically in a rude manner
5.	deft	_____	e.	to deliberately destroy or damage public or private property

Sentences: Try to use the words above in a sentence below. Remember that a word ending may be changed or its figure of speech slightly altered.

6. There is little _____ for someone to work a job without either salary or the ability to develop specific career skills.

7. Marianne is a(n) _____ musician and is able to play several brass and woodwind instruments with ease.

8. The spectators _____ at Ryan after he missed his final field goal and lost the football game.

9. After mooring their ships in the harbor, pirates _____ the city of St. Augustine.

10. That Brian had had an accident at lunch was _____ obvious: he returned in the afternoon with a big spaghetti sauce stain on his otherwise immaculate white shirt.

NEW WORDS

mature
mə'CHoŏr, -'t(y)oŏr

malign
mə'līn

fortify
'fôrtə,fī

murky
'mərkē

caprice
kə'prēs

Lesson 50

A WILL OF ONE'S OWN

Growing up, Lucy and Emily's aunt Euridice regularly lectured them in a disparaging tone about the necessity of securing a wealthy, educated husband. Now at **mature** ages, Lucy and Emily no longer allow their aunt to **malign** them with **murky** rhetoric about the prospect of marriage. Preferring to remain single and enjoy a young adulthood of **caprice**, the girls do not even think of dating. In their opinion, no man can **fortify** their lives: only by following their passions can they find true happiness and inner meaning.

Definitions: Try matching the words in the list with the appropriate definitions. If you are stuck, check the glossary in the back of the book or the passage at the top of the page.

1.   mature   _____   a.   (adj.) fully developed physically; full-grown; (v.) to become physically or emotionally developed

2.   malign   _____   b.   to strengthen a place with defensive works so as to protect it from attack; to strengthen or invigorate someone mentally or physically

3.   fortify   _____   c.   (adj.) evil in nature or effect, malevolent; (v.) to speak about another in a spitefully cruel manner

4.   murky   _____   d.   dark and gloomy, usually because of thick mist

5.   caprice   _____   e.   a sudden and unaccountable change of mood or behavior

Sentences: Try to use the words above in a sentence below. Remember that a word ending may be changed or its figure of speech slightly altered.

6.   Taylor, who is very steadfast, has very little patience for people who are _____ and thus change their mind erratically.

7.   It takes a(n) _____ person to be able to take responsibility for his or her actions.

8.   Extra beams were added to the building's frame in order to _____ it.

9.   Often in a political campaign, candidates attempt to _____ their opponents in an attempt to gain support.

10.   Haunted places often are situated in a(n) _____ ambiance at night.

Word Search

Lessons 41-50

```
L S U O M Y N O N A M E A G E R D
T D M Z Q T R N P Y P R Y R M R Q
U R R R C K T Y P J Y C U L G G R
R A Q I N O E P N R R T V D T M V
B W T T N E N E R E A N Y M Z N B
U B Y Z N E V T M M Y Y T J T D B
L A G L F E V I R N R U T I C A T
E C J E Y X G U T I R G B P M P M
N K R B R T Y R O N B E L P N M Y
T A W W L H N N U S E U T I K J V
L Y K Q P A E U G S T C T S N L N
M N K O Y D T Q O I N Q N E D T Z
Q J R W A J N A T B L I N I D B Q
T T T V J J Y D N V R A X B Y L Q
A J N D G B L Z M T D Y M Y T T N
Y I X K X X M G N K L D T N G Z W
```

1 (adj.) characterized by conflict, disorder, or confusion; liquid that moves violently and unsteadily
2 (adj.) describing a person who is serious and unrelenting, especially in matters of assertion of authority and exertion of discipline; strict and severe; (n.) the rearmost part of a ship or boat
3 (adj.) lacking in quantity or quality
4 (adj.) rising in active revolt; (n.) a rebel or revolutionary
5 (adj.) a thing kept as a reminder of a person, place, or event
6 (adj.) quiet, gentle, submissive; easily imposed upon
7 (adj.) (usually of an animal) in a wild state, especially after escaping domesticity or captivity
8 (v.) 1. for a body tissue to waste away, typically due to the degeneration of cells; 2. to gradually decline in effectiveness or vigor due to underuse or neglect
9 (adj.) (of a person) not identified by name, or of unknown name
10 (v.) to give (something, often money) in order to help achieve or provide something
11 (n.) 1. generosity, liberality; abundance; 2.

a monetary gift or reward given by a government, usually for killing or capturing a criminal
12 (n.) a feature that renders something less acceptable; a disadvantage or problem
13 (n.) compassion or forgiveness shown toward someone whom it is within one's power to punish or harm
14 (v.) for an armed forces to enter a region and occupy it; to enter an area in large numbers; for a disease to spread into an organism or body part; to encroach or intrude on
15 (adj.) a person who is reserved and uncommunicative in speech; saying little
16 (n.) a small flash of light; (of one's eyes) a shine with a particular emotion; (v.) to give out or reflect small flashes of light
17 (adj.) typically bad behavior done openly and unashamedly
18 (n.) a thing that motivates or encourages one to do something
19 (adj.) fully developed physically; full-grown; (v.) to become physically or emotionally developed
20 (adj.) evil in nature or effect, malevolent; (v.) to speak about another in a spitefully cruel manner

Vocabulary Review
Lessons 41-50

Directions: Match each word with its best approximate definition. Note
that definitions are not necessarily repeated verbatim from the
lesson exercises.

1.	uncanny	_____	a.	quarrelsome; combative
2.	upbraid	_____	b.	easily bent or influenced; flexible
3.	debris	_____	c.	extremely complex or detailed
4.	intricate	_____	d.	dark and gloomy, often due to thick mist
5.	pugnacious	_____	e.	many and various
6.	burnish	_____	f.	to make rude, often loud, mocking remarks
7.	robust	_____	g.	to exist at an earlier point in time than something
8.	pliable	_____	h.	to deliberately destroy or damage something (usually public property)
9.	modicum	_____	i.	scattered fragments remaining after something has been wrecked or destroyed
10.	cosmic	_____	j.	a panicked rush of horses (or cattle or other animals)
11.	deter	_____	k.	relating to the universe, especially as distinct from Earth
12.	predate	_____	l.	a sequence of actions regularly followed; a fixed program
13.	routine	_____	m.	strong and healthy; vigorous
14.	stampede	_____	n.	strange or mysterious, especially in an unsettling way
15.	manifold	_____	o.	to scold or find fault with someone
16.	communicate	_____	p.	to strengthen or invigorate
17.	jeer	_____	q.	to polish
18.	vandalize	_____	r.	a very small amount
19.	fortify	_____	s.	to exchange information, news, or ideas
20.	murky	_____	t.	to discourage someone from doing something

Word Roots: Unit 5

ROOTS AND THEIR MEANINGS

path:	feeling	cred:	believe
uni/mono:	one	circ/circum:	around
cog(n)	to know	ac/acr:	sharp, bitter

Here are a few examples of some words that use the above roots:

empathy: the ability to understand and share the feelings of another
unicycle: a cycle with one wheel, often used by circus entertainers or acrobats
monocle: a single eyeglass that one wears
cognitive: related to thinking or the mind
incredible: hard to believe; unbelievable
circumvent: to find a way around an obstacle
acerbic: sharp and forthright; bitter or sour tasting

Now try to fill in the table below by finding the appropriate root(s) and interpreting the meaning of each word:

Word	Root(s)	Guessed Meaning	Actual Meaning
sociopath			
uniform (adj.)			
circumnavigate			
credibility			
acrid			
incredulous			
credulous			
acrimonious			
monochrome			
recognize			
incognito			
circumlocution			
circumspect			

Specific Vocabularies I
Animal Words

While the standard lessons in this book contain words frequently used in intellectual and academic English, it is also important to realize that certain careers and disciplines have their own specific vocabularies. Many individuals know some words from specific vocabularies, but they may not know a majority of them. Often it is helpful to know such words to be more conversant in specific fields, and some of them may appear frequently on exams with analogy sections. In this book, we aim to furnish you with some specific vocabularies to aid your vocabulary growth.

Words for Groups of Animals:

- A group of dogs or wolves is called a **pack**
- A group of cats is called a **clowder**
- A group of baby cats is called a **litter**
- A group of fish is called a **school**
- A group of crows is called a **murder**
- A group of birds (in general) is called a **flock**
- A group of lions is called a **pride**
- A group of monkeys is called a **troop** or **cartload**
- A group of bees is called a **swarm**
- A group of buffalo, moose, buffalo, ox, deer, sheep, yak, alpaca, or cattle is called a **herd**
- A sudden panicked rush of horses or other cattle is called a **stampede**

Words for Baby Animals:

- A baby dog is called a **pup (puppy)**
- A baby cat is called a **kitten**
- A baby kangaroo is called a **joey**
- A baby goat is called a **kid**
- A baby pig is called a **piglet**
- A baby bear is called a **cub**
- A baby sheep is called a **lamb**, **lambkin**, or **cosset**

Some Male and Female Animal Terms:

- A male chicken is called a **rooster**

- A female chicken is called a **hen**
- A male deer is often called a **buck** or **stag**
- A female deer is often called a **doe**
- A baby male horse is called a **colt**
- A baby female horse is called a **filly**

Words for Enclosures Containing Certain Animals:

- A large cage or enclosure for keeping birds in is called an **aviary**
- A place where bees are kept is called an **apiary**
- A place that bees construct as a locus of activity is called a **hive**
- A place that hornets or wasps construct as a locus of activity is called a **nest**
- A cage or pen confining poultry is called a **coop**
- An enclosure for pigs is a **sty** or **pen**

Terms to Describe Category or Likeness of an Animal:

- The term **canine** concerns something of, relating to, or resembling a dog or dogs
- The term **feline** concerns something of, relating to, or resembling a cat or cats, or members of the cat family
- The term **vulpine** concerns something of, relating to, or resembling a fox or foxes
- The term **lupine** concerns something of, relating to, or resembling a wolf or wolves
- The term **porcine** concerns something of, relating to, affecting, or resembling a pig or pigs
- The term **bovine** concerns something of, relating to, or resembling a cattle (especially cows)
- The term **piscine** concerns something of, relating to, or resembling a fish or fish

Some Miscellaneous Animal Terms:

- The process of change or transformation by which a caterpillar becomes a butterfly or a tadpole becomes a frog is called **metamorphosis**
- An informal term referring to a dead animal that has been hit by a vehicle (often on a highway or high-speed road) is called **road kill**
- The claw on a bird of prey is called a **talon**
- The needles on a porcupine used for self-defense are called **quills**
- A small horse is called a **pony**
- An animal with a backbone is called a **vertebrate**
- An animal lacking a backbone is called an **invertebrate**

NEW WORDS

plausible
ˈplôzəbəl

devoted
diˈvōtid

amble
ˈambəl

gale
gāl

crude
kro͞od

It was sunny outside and perfect for a pleasant **amble** along the beach, so the young couple decided to go to the coast for the afternoon. Though they were **devoted** parents, they felt this beautiful weather provided the perfect opportunity to spend some time by themselves. Two hours later, they were finally walking down the narrow stony beach. Suddenly the clouds gathered; a strong **gale** and pouring rain followed seconds later. The couple ran and hid under a **crude** shelter made of fallen branches. It was **plausible** that the summer storm would be short; therefore, they kept their high spirits while looking at the water.

Definitions: Try matching the words in the list with the appropriate definitions. If you are stuck, check the glossary in the back of the book or the passage at the top of the page.

1.	plausible	_____	a.	to walk or move at a slow, relaxed pace
2.	devoted	_____	b.	very loving and loyal
3.	amble	_____	c.	an argument or statement that seems reasonable or logical
4.	gale	_____	d.	1. in a natural or raw state; unrefined; 2. constructed in a rudimentary way; 3. (of a person) especially offensive or rude, especially in a sexual way
5.	crude	_____	e.	a very strong wind

Sentences: Try to use the words above in a sentence below. Remember that a word ending may be changed or its figure of speech slightly altered.

6. Kenneth _____ his way to the country club gate and greeted the guests.

7. Gerald's _____ language alienated his superiors, who refused to work with him.

8. It is difficult to guide a boat through a(n) _____: often a strong wind will cause a boat to capsize.

9. Jake is so _____ to his career that he sleeps and showers in a room right above his restaurant.

10. That James was late to work because his car broke down is indeed a(n) _____ excuse for his tardiness.

Lesson 52

THE TURNAROUND

The **cupidity** of the new company director would eventually **erode** the company's moral principles. Gradually, money became the sole motivating agent in everyone's actions. While the atmosphere had been **placid** and warm before, now there was a **thorough** turnaround in the employees' relationships. The company kept up the **fiction** that everything was going as usual, but soon clients could see deterioration in the quality of its products.

NEW WORDS

cupidity
kyoō'piditē

thorough
'THərō

placid
'plasid

fiction
'fikSHən

erode
i'rōd

Definitions: Try matching the words in the list with the appropriate definitions. If you are stuck, check the glossary in the back of the book or the passage at the top of the page.

1.	cupidity	_____	a.	prose literature in the form of novels that describes imaginary people and events
2.	thorough	_____	b.	a person or animal not easily upset or excited; (of a place or stretch of water) calm and peaceful, with little movement or activity
3.	placid	_____	c.	greed for money or possessions
4.	fiction	_____	d.	to gradually wear away (usually of water, wind, or other natural elements)
5.	erode	_____	e.	complete with regard to every detail

Sentences: Try to use the words above in a sentence below. Remember that a word ending may be changed or its figure of speech slightly altered.

6. That there were once unicorns in Asia is indeed _____: unicorns have never existed!

7. Though the waters on Kebo Lake are usually rough, today they are uncharacteristically _____.

8. Dr. Park did a(n) _____ job of critiquing my paper and provided detailed feedback on both my writing and its footnotes.

9. While having money is important, Laura's _____ made her friends think that it was the *raison d'être* of her existence.

10. Over time the Colorado River _____ land in Northern Arizona, thus helping form the Grand Canyon.

NEW WORDS

concede
kənˈsēd

tact
takt

nonessential
ˌnänəˈsenCHəl

terrestrial
təˈrestrēəl, -ˈresCHəl

bide
bīd

Lesson 53

THE QUASI GURU

He was considered a highly spiritual man but, at the **terrestrial** level, he often showed a lack of **tact** and offended the people around him. His devotees would **bide** their time near him because they believed he was a holy man. They saw his insults as **nonessential** compared to the great wisdom that they believed he imparted to them. They would never **concede** that, in truth, he was simply a grumpy old man with some charisma and an inflated ego.

Definitions: Try matching the words in the list with the appropriate definitions. If you are stuck, check the glossary in the back of the book or the passage at the top of the page.

1.	concede	_____	a.	not absolutely necessary
2.	tact	_____	b.	1. to admit that something is true or valid after first denying or resisting it; 2. to surrender or yield something that one possesses or desires
3.	nonessential	_____	c.	sensitivity in dealing with others or with difficult issues
4.	terrestrial	_____	d.	relating to the land or the Earth
5.	bide	_____	e.	to remain or stay somewhere

Sentences: Try to use the words above in a sentence below. Remember that a word ending may be changed or its figure of speech slightly altered.

6. After a hard fought campaign, it was difficult for the losing candidate to _____ the election to her opponent.

7. Paul's lack of _____ has repulsed many of his friends, who have been personally insulted by his directness.

8. Humans are _____ creatures: they dwell and work on the land.

9. Green food coloring is a(n) _____ ingredient in the recipe to make mint ice cream.

10. Joanna _____ her time at the beach while her sister was selling tacos downtown.

81

Lesson 54

ATTEMPTING TO NARRATE A CRIME

The police asked the victim to **narrate** the crime. Unfortunately, it was so **odious** to the victim that he could hardly speak without crying. Remembering that night filled him with anger and **anxiety**. As he told his story, he put the **emphasis** on the intense emotional pain that he had to bear. There was a **consensus** among the police officers that the victim was too emotionally jarred at that moment to talk, so they waited a few days before interrogating him again.

NEW WORDS

anxiety
aNG'zī-itē

consensus
kən'sensəs

emphasis
'emfəsis

narrate
'nar͵āt

odious
'ōdēəs

Definitions: Try matching the words in the list with the appropriate definitions. If you are stuck, check the glossary in the back of the book or the passage at the top of the page.

1.	anxiety	_____	a.	a general agreement
2.	consensus	_____	b.	special importance, value, or prominence given to something
3.	emphasis	_____	c.	a feeling of worry, unease, or nervousness, typically about an imminent event or one with an uncertain outcome
4.	narrate	_____	d.	extremely unpleasant; repulsive
5.	odious	_____	e.	to give a spoken or written account of something

Sentences: Try to use the words above in a sentence below. Remember that a word ending may be changed or its figure of speech slightly altered.

6.   If a charismatic person is chosen to _____ the tale, its message will resonate more potently with the audience.

7.   Leslie has a great fear of theme park rides, so it was no surprise that he had great _____ about getting in line to ride a giant roller coaster.

8.   There is a general _____ in America that getting a college education will aid one's career prospects.

9.   While some mathematics books choose to highlight drills and practice problems, the _____ of this one is on conceptual understanding.

10.   Many faculty members in the law school find the head secretary to be a disorganized and _____ person.

NEW WORDS

allay
əˈlā

animosity
ˌanəˈmäsitē

destitute
ˈdestiˌt(y)o͞ot

catastrophe
ˈkəˈtastrəfē

proficient
prəˈfiSHənt

CHOOSING A PATH IN LIFE

Shanine lived in a poor neighborhood with many **destitute** children walking on the streets. The sight of their sad faces and torn clothes broke her heart. She often gave them food in order to **allay** their hunger. She felt a certain **animosity** in them, as if they didn't completely trust her. To her, that loss of childhood innocence was a **catastrophe**. She decided that when she goes to college, she will study social work and become more **proficient** at helping such children — this became her life goal.

Definitions: Try matching the words in the list with the appropriate definitions. If you are stuck, check the glossary in the back of the book or the passage at the top of the page.

1. allay _____ a. an event causing great and often sudden damage or suffering
2. animosity _____ b. (of a fear, suspicion, or worry) to diminish or put at rest
3. destitute _____ c. competent or skilled in doing or using something
4. catastrophe _____ d. lacking the basic necessities in life
5. proficient _____ e. strong hostility

Sentences: Try to use the words above in a sentence below. Remember that a word ending may be changed or its figure of speech slightly altered.

6. Because Frieda had not saved any money during her career, she found herself almost _____ upon retirement.
7. It is unfortunate when there is _____ between a child's parents during a divorce: often such harsh feelings can cause serious emotional damage to the child.
8. Three tornadoes swept through town causing a great _____.
9. If one is not _____ in the English language, it will be difficult to succeed at an American university.
10. Unfortunately, Donna could to little to _____ Leslie's fear of heights: Leslie refused to go to the top of the skyscraper despite all of Donna's efforts.

Lesson 56

A BLEAK FUTURE

As his health was quickly deteriorating, the king became more lethargic and irritable. He dismissed his responsibilities as **banal** and tedious tasks, he often drifted in a fitful **doze** during the day, and he did not hesitate to **banish** those who opposed his decisions. Since there was no suitable inheritor to the throne, **domestic** violence between factions to gain political power was inevitable. The fate of the kingdom was placed in grave **jeopardy.**

NEW WORDS

domestic
də'mestik

banal
'bānl, bə'nal, -'näl

banish
'baniSH

doze
dōz

jeopardy
'jepərdē

Definitions: Try matching the words in the list with the appropriate definitions. If you are stuck, check the glossary in the back of the book or the passage at the top of the page.

1.	domestic	_____	a.	1. of or relating to running a home or family relations; 2. existing or occurring inside a particular country
2.	banal	_____	b.	lacking in originality and thus being obvious or boring
3.	banish	_____	c.	to send someone away from a country or place as official punishment
4.	doze	_____	d.	to sleep lightly
5.	jeopardy	_____	e.	danger of loss, harm, or failure

Sentences: Try to use the words above in a sentence below. Remember that a word ending may be changed or its figure of speech slightly altered.

6. The queen _____ the traitor from her kingdom after he and his comrades plotted to kill her.

7. Telling high school graduates that they are the future of the world is a rather _____ statement.

8. I am more concerned with _____ issues such as tax rates and racial equality than with international politics.

9. Many Europeans enjoy taking a(n) _____ in the middle of the afternoon to refresh them for evening work.

10. Bertha's life was put in _____ when the brakes on her motorbike suddenly failed her.

NEW WORDS

yearn
yərn

facilitate
fəˈsiliˌtāt

fruitful
ˈfro͞otfəl

awkward
ˈôkwərd

boycott
ˈboiˌkät

Lesson 57

DEFENDING ONE'S RIGHTS

Employees for the national airline have announced that they are going on strike following the company's **awkward** and unfair decision to cut salaries by 40% in response to the recent drop in revenue. Consequently, two airline workers' unions have convened to find a strategy defending rights to fair payment for the workers. The union delegates **yearn** to reach to an agreement that will **facilitate** a **fruitful** resolution to these problems. If such a resolution cannot be reached, chances are high that customers may **boycott** the airlines because of its unfair worker treatment.

Definitions: Try matching the words in the list with the appropriate definitions. If you are stuck, check the glossary in the back of the book or the passage at the top of the page.

1.   yearn   _____   a.   producing much fruit, fertile; producing good or helpful results

2.   facilitate   _____   b.   1. causing difficulty, hard to do or deal with; 2. causing or feeling embarrassment or inconvenience; 3. not smooth or grateful

3.   fruitful   _____   c.   to make an action or process easier

4.   awkward   _____   d.   (n.) a punitive ban that forbids relations with certain groups, cooperation with a policy, or the handling of goods; (v.) to withdraw from commercial or social relations with a country, organization, or person as punishment or protest

5.   boycott   _____   e.   to have an intense feeling of longing for something or someone, especially if one is separated from it

Sentences: Try to use the words above in a sentence below. Remember that a word ending may be changed or its figure of speech slightly altered.

6.   Unfortunately, I am unable to _____ in helping you transition into a new career as I lack both the skills and the time to commit.

7.   Many girls _____ to become princesses and live happily ever after.

8.   Often the best way to demonstrate against a company's abuses is to _____ that company's products.

9.   There was a(n) _____ silence when Meghan's fiancé let out a loud, stinky fart at the dinner table.

10. It is not _____ to lament the past when such energy can be devoted to building an amazing future.

Lesson 58

LIFE CHANGES

Jackson had tremendous **stamina**, so moving to a place by the ocean with a different climate did not bother him. At first he was fine with the **humidity** and the permanent sweating. However, he had a **penchant** for drinking and he felt extra dehydrated after a night out partying. He began to experience a tiredness that **debilitated** his ability to concentrate for long time periods. He was no longer able to focus on something as **trivial** as a brief newscast.

NEW WORDS

stamina
ˈstamənə

humidity
(h)yoōˈmiditē

penchant
ˈpenCHənt

debilitate
diˈbiliˌtāt, dē-

trivial
ˈtrivēəl

Definitions: Try matching the words in the list with the appropriate definitions. If you are stuck, check the glossary in the back of the book or the passage at the top of the page.

1.	stamina	_____	a.	a strong and habitual liking for something or tendency to do something
2.	humidity	_____	b.	concerning the amount of water vapor in the air
3.	penchant	_____	c.	1. to make someone weak and infirm; 2. to hinder, delay, or weaken
4.	debilitate	_____	d.	of little value or importance; (of a person) concerned only with trifling or unimportant things
5.	trivial	_____	e.	the ability to sustain prolonged physical or mental effort

Sentences: Try to use the words above in a sentence below. Remember that a word ending may be changed or its figure of speech slightly altered.

6. I wish I had the _____ that I had twenty years ago; I do not think I could still run a marathon at my age.

7. Kimberly always had a(n) _____ for cooking, so it is only natural that she has tried to establish herself as a chef in a luxury restaurant downtown.

8. Understanding Einstein's Theory of Relativity is no _____ matter; the concepts involved are quite intricate and advanced.

9. Unfortunately an automobile accident ten years ago left my uncle _____; that is why he occasionally needs a wheelchair.

10. Rainforests are noted to have climates with high _____ because they have regular precipitation.

NEW WORDS

allege
əˈlej

abase
əˈbās

bulge
bəlj

adage
ˈadij

familial
fəˈmilēəl, -ˈmilyəl

CORRUPTION EXPOSED

His opponent sought to **allege** that Senator Sam took substantial sums of money in bribes and used his **familial** and political connections to buy his son a governmental job. Sam insisted that he would not **abase** himself by admitting a crime he did not commit. An investigation, however, soon confirmed the accusations. Meanwhile, his son also got caught shoplifting when an employee noticed an unusual **bulge** in his pocket. As the old **adage** goes, "Like father, like son" — both Sam and his son were imprisoned for their greed.

Definitions: Try matching the words in the list with the appropriate definitions. If you are stuck, check the glossary in the back of the book or the passage at the top of the page.

1.	allege	_____	a. (n.) a rounded swelling or protuberance that distorts a flat surface; (v.) to swell or protrude to an unnatural or incongruous extent
2.	abase	_____	b. to behave in such a way as to degrade or belittle someone
3.	bulge	_____	c. a proverb or short statement expressing a general truth
4.	adage	_____	d. of, relating to, or concerning a family and its members
5.	familial	_____	e. to claim or assert that someone has done something illegal or wrong, typically without proof

Sentences: Try to use the words above in a sentence below. Remember that a word ending may be changed or its figure of speech slightly altered.

6. Discussions concerning personal finances are more often than not _____ matters.

7. A(n) old _____ goes, "A penny saved is a penny earned."

8. It is easy to _____ that my landlord stole money out of my room because he is the only person I know with a key to the front door.

9. Typically when a woman is pregnant, one can recognize an obvious _____ in her stomach.

10. Despite being thrown out of graduate school, Oriana did not _____ her reputation with colleagues at other universities.

Lesson 60

THE MAN WITH A GUN

The **putrid** smell coming from the basement indicated that there was rotten meat below. It was against the law to kill animals in that mountainous region, and the police officer had a **legitimate** reason to check the smell. However, he remained **calm** and did not say a word. He saw that the owner of the house had a crazed look in his eyes; the owner looked unstable and was holding a gun. Caution, or perhaps **cowardice**, overcame the police officer and he backed away. The officer realized that government authorities needed to **reform** the law and do background checks on the people that want to buy a gun.

Definitions: Try matching the words in the list with the appropriate definitions. If you are stuck, check the glossary in the back of the book or the passage at the top of the page.

1. reform _____   a. (adj.) conforming to the law or rules; (v.) to justify or make lawful

2. legitimate _____   b. (n.) the action of making changes in something (typically a social, political, or economic institution or practice) in order to improve it (v.) to make changes in something (typically a social, political, or economic institution or practice) in order to improve it

3. cowardice _____   c. (adj.) 1. (of a person) not showing signs of anger, nervousness, or other emotions, 2. pleasantly free from wind; (n.) 1. the absence of violent confrontational activity within a place or group; 2. the absence of wind; (v.) to make someone quiet; soothe

4. calm _____   d. lack of bravery

5. putrid _____   e. characteristic of rotting matter and having a foul smell

Sentences: Try to use the words above in a sentence below. Remember that a word ending may be changed or its figure of speech slightly altered.

6.   One of my father's best attributes is that he is able to keep _____ in the midst of unsettling events.

7.   After fifty successful years, the Italian restaurant is looking to _____ some of its business practices.

8.   Elaine's _____ rendered her too timid to take risks and speak out.

9.   It often can be tough to tell if a signature is _____ or is a forgery.

10.   Because Brad did not empty his trash, a(n) _____ smell filled the room.

Crossword Puzzle
Lessons 51-60

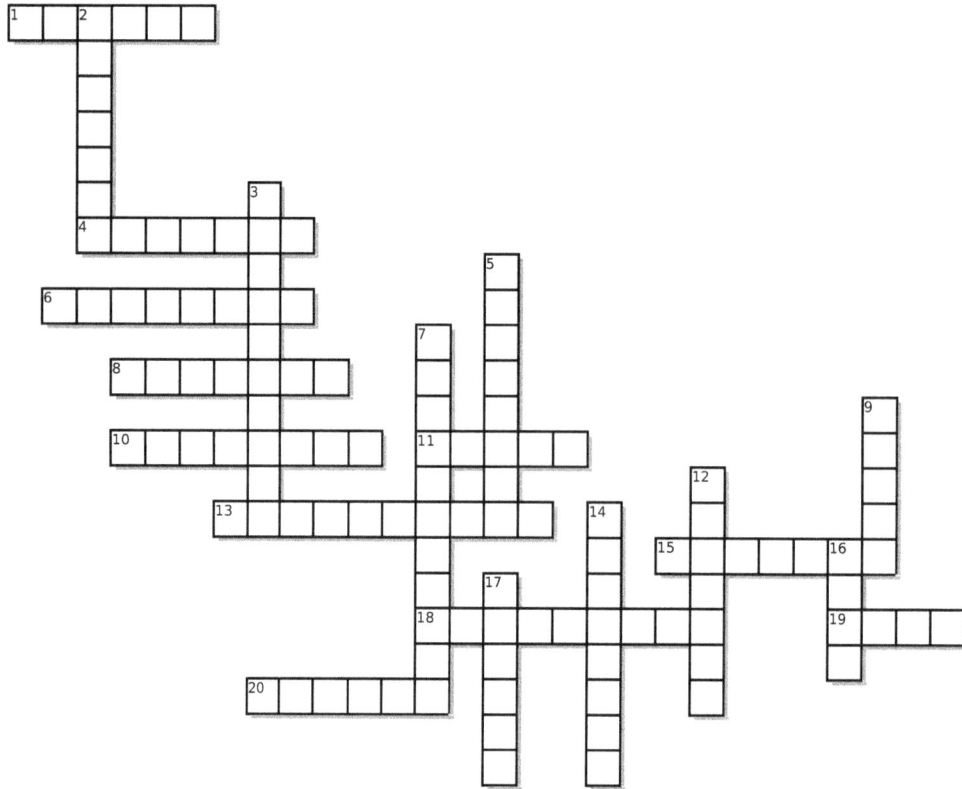

ACROSS

1 (adj.) a person or animal not easily upset or excited; (of a place or stretch of water) calm and peaceful, with little movement or activity
4 (adj.) very loving and loyal
6 (adj.) 1. of or relating to running a home or family relations; 2. existing or occurring inside a particular country
8 (n.) prose literature in the form of novels that describes imaginary people and events
10 (n.) special importance, value, or prominence given to something
11 (v.) to behave in such a way as to degrade or belittle someone
13 (adj.) 1. to make someone weak and infirm; 2. to hinder, delay, or weaken
15 (n.) a feeling of worry, unease, or nervousness, typically about an imminent event or one with an uncertain outcome
18 (adj.) an argument or statement that seems reasonable or logical
19 (adj.) 1. (of a person) not showing signs of anger, nervousness, or other emotions, 2. pleasantly free from wind; (n.) 1. the absence of violent confrontational activity within a place or group; 2.

the absence of wind; (v.) to make someone quiet; soothe
20 (v.) to claim or assert that someone has done something illegal or wrong, typically without proof

DOWN

2 (adj.) 1. causing difficulty, hard to do or deal with; 2. causing or feeling embarrassment or inconvenience; 3. not smooth or grateful
3 (adj.) conforming to the law or rules; (v.) to justify or make lawful
5 (n.) a strong and habitual liking for something or tendency to do something
7 (n.) an event causing great and often sudden damage or suffering
9 (v.) (of a fear, suspicion, or worry) to diminish or put at rest
12 (v.) 1. to admit that something is true or valid after first denying or resisting it; 2. to surrender or yield something that one possesses
14 (adj.) producing much fruit, fertile; producing good or helpful results
16 (n.) sensitivity in dealing with others or with difficult issues
17 (v.) to send someone away from a country or place as official punishment

Vocabulary Review
Lessons 51-60

Directions: Match each word with its best approximate definition. Note that definitions are not necessarily repeated verbatim from the lesson exercises.

1.	amble	_____	a.	not absolutely necessary
2.	gale	_____	b.	greed for possessions or money
3.	cupidity	_____	c.	decaying or rotting and giving of a foul smell
4.	thorough	_____	d.	to have an intense feeling of longing for something, often that one has been separated from
5.	nonessential	_____	e.	to give a spoken or written account of something
6.	terrestrial	_____	f.	concerning the amount of water vapor present in the air
7.	consensus	_____	g.	lacking the basic necessities of life
8.	narrate	_____	h.	to walk or move slowly and with relaxation
9.	animosity	_____	i.	the ability to sustain mental or physical effort
10.	destitute	_____	j.	lacking in originality; boring
11.	banal	_____	k.	exhibiting a lack of bravery
12.	jeopardy	_____	l.	on, of, or relating to the earth
13.	yearn	_____	m.	a general agreement
14.	facilitate	_____	n.	strong hostility
15.	stamina	_____	o.	concerning a family and its members
16.	humidity	_____	p.	to make an action or process easy or easier
17.	adage	_____	q.	complete with regard to all details
18.	familial	_____	r.	a proverb or short saying expressing a general truth
19.	cowardice	_____	s.	a very strong wind
20.	putrid	_____	t.	danger of failure, harm, or loss

Word Roots: Unit 6

ROOTS AND THEIR MEANINGS

dys:	faulty, bad	mal:	bad
homo:	same	mis:	wrong, bad
hetero:	different	vers/vert:	to turn
pan:	everywhere, all	ab/abs:	away from, against

Here are a few examples of some words that use the above roots:

dystopia:	an imagined place where everything is bad; the opposite of a utopia
homophone:	each of two words having the same pronunciation, but with different meanings and spellings
heterosexual:	a person sexually attracted to people of the opposite sex
pantheon:	all the gods of a religion collectively; a building where the dead of a nation are collectively honored
maladjusted:	failing to adapt to the demands of a normal social environment
misanthrope:	a person who dislikes mankind and who shuns society
vertigo:	a sensation of dizziness or loss of balance, often when looking down from heights
aberration:	an anomaly or departure from what is normally expected

Now try to fill in the table below by finding the appropriate root(s) and interpreting the meaning of each word:

Word	Root(s)	Guessed Meaning	Actual Meaning
abstain			
dysfunction			
homogeneous			
heterodox			
malign			
panacea			
averse			

misnomer			
heterogeneous			
pandemonium			
dyslexic			
maladroit			
mistake			
absolve			
abnegate			

NEW WORDS

somber
ˈsämbər

tardy
ˈtärdē

subdue
səbˈd(y)o͞o

oath
ō TH

cultivate
ˈkəltəˌvāt

Lesson 61

LIFE'S TRIBULATIONS

Nothing could **subdue** Ronald's pain after he was fired from his job. He walked around with a **somber** expression and became **tardy** in doing even the simplest household tasks. Sometimes, instead of responding to a question, he would just utter an **oath** and become silent again. The rest of Ronald's family had to **cultivate** patience in order to deal with his new behavior, but soon he became too unbearable for everyone and they asked him to move out.

Definitions: Try matching the words in the list with the appropriate definitions. If you are stuck, check the glossary in the back of the book or the passage at the top of the page.

1. somber _____ a. a solemn promise, often invoking a divine witness, regarding one's future behavior or action

2. tardy _____ b. to overcome, calm, or bring under control (a feeling or person)

3. subdue _____ c. dark or dull in color and tone; gloomy

4. oath _____ d. 1. to prepare and use land for crops or gardening; 2. to acquire and develop a quality, skill, or sentiment

5. cultivate _____ e. delaying or delayed beyond the expected time; late

Sentences: Try to use the words above in a sentence below. Remember that a word ending may be changed or its figure of speech slightly altered.

6. Attending a funeral is typically a(n) _____ affair.

7. Jerome is often _____ to class; he usually disrupts lecture when he arrives.

8. In the United States, a new President initially must take a(n) _____ before being able to exercise his or her power.

9. Marla has the amazing ability to _____ a bunch of rowdy kindergarteners and to have them listen to her.

10. Cressida enjoys _____ plants in her new vegetable garden.

Lesson 62

SERIAL KILLERS

There seem to be certain similarities in the behavior of serial killers. They often **foster** feelings of intense hate towards a certain community, occasionally accompanied by **furious** angry outbursts. They can be **presumptuous** and feel that the world owes them something. They are capable of committing **heinous** murders and can exhibit **brazen** indifference towards what a victim's relatives say in court. The mentality of such people remains a mystery to many people, which may be the reason for a growing number of documentaries and television shows on the subject.

NEW WORDS

foster
ˈfôstər, ˈfäs-

presumptuous
priˈzəmpCH(o͞o)əs

furious
ˈfyo͝orēəs

heinous
ˈhānəs

brazen
ˈbrāzən

Definitions: Try matching the words in the list with the appropriate definitions. If you are stuck, check the glossary in the back of the book or the passage at the top of the page.

1.   foster   _____   a.   (concerning a person and his or her behavior) failing to observe the limits of what is deemed appropriate

2.   presumptuous _____   b.   a person, wrongful act, or crime that is utterly odious or wicked

3.   furious   _____   c.   extremely angry

4.   heinous   _____   d.   to encourage or promote the development of something; to develop a feeling or idea within oneself

5.   brazen   _____   e.   bold and without shame

Sentences: Try to use the words above in a sentence below. Remember that a word ending may be changed or its figure of speech slightly altered.

6.   Diana was _____ enough to raise her hand in an auditorium of a thousand people and ask the famous movie director for an internship.

7.   Mario acted _____ when he assumed his student was not doing work before checking in with the student first.

8.   When Marilyn's mom heard that her daughter had absconded and gotten married, she was _____.

9.   Lynching, slavery, and segregation are among the many _____ actions plaguing the history of the American South.

10.   Providing young children with good mentors and books is an important part of _____ their education.

94

Lesson 63

FUELED BY NATIONALISM

After the war, the country finally escaped from the grip of its colonizer and became a **sovereign** nation. Most celebrated the nation's hard-won independence, but any individual who once fawned over the enemy was treated like a **pariah** and traitor in the community. While the local citizens would often bully and **pester** such individuals with disparaging remarks, the government also **imposed** a stricter control on them. From limiting their property rights to banning them from holding important positions, the new order slowly **ensnared** those who worked for the past colonial government.

Definitions: Try matching the words in the list with the appropriate definitions. If you are stuck, check the glossary in the back of the book or the passage at the top of the page.

1.	pariah	_____	a.	an outcast
2.	sovereign	_____	b.	1. to force something unwelcome or unfamiliar to be accepted or put into place; 2. to take advantage of someone by demanding their attention or commitment
3.	impose	_____	c.	to trouble or annoy someone with frequent interruptions or requests
4.	pester	_____	d.	to catch in or as in a trap
5.	ensnare	_____	e.	(adj.) possessing supreme or ultimate power; (n.) a supreme ruler, especially a monarch

Sentences: Try to use the words above in a sentence below. Remember that a word ending may be changed or its figure of speech slightly altered.

6.   Ellen _____ the local handyman almost daily by demanding that he look at problems in her home.

7.   The pretty girl's charisma was not enough to _____ Harry into dating her.

8.   Attempting to _____ a tax on cigarettes is one approach to helping curb a smoking epidemic.

9.   The Queen of England is able to rule over her subjects because it is her _____ right to do so.

10.   Pamela did not dress like the other people in her department, and so she was treated like a(n) _____ at many events.

Lesson 64

THE SMALL PROVINCIAL THEATER

When the actress accidentally stumbled and fell, the theater broke out in **boisterous** laughter. The audience showed no **compassion** for her; in fact, they welcomed the mishap. After a hard day of work in the factories, the men in the audience could not **omit** the chance to have a laugh at her expense. In fact, whenever they did not like something in the play, the men would hurl **acrid** remarks at the cast. Such casual behavior was certainly **repugnant** to the spirit of theater performances in the city; however, it was the norm in this small industrial town.

> ## NEW WORDS
>
> **boisterous**
> ˈboist(ə)rəs
>
> **omit**
> ōˈmit
>
> **acrid**
> ˈakrid
>
> **repugnant**
> riˈpəgnənt
>
> **compassion**
> kəmˈpaSHən

Definitions: Try matching the words in the list with the appropriate definitions. If you are stuck, check the glossary in the back of the book or the passage at the top of the page.

1. boisterous _____ a. having an irritatingly strong and unpleasant taste or smell

2. omit _____ b. 1. (of a person, event, or occasion) energetic, noisy, and cheerful; 2. (of wind, weather, or water) wild or stormy

3. acrid _____ c. to leave out or exclude, either intentionally or deliberately

4. repugnant _____ d. extremely distasteful; unacceptable

5. compassion _____ e. sympathetic pity and concern for the suffering and misfortunes of others

Sentences: Try to use the words above in a sentence below. Remember that a word ending may be changed or its figure of speech slightly altered.

6. Always the life of the party, Curran can turn a subdued atmosphere into a(n) _____ one.

7. Most educators should be strict with their students, but it is also important to be stern with _____: criticism should be balanced with an equal amount of care.

8. The lemon chicken looks excellent, but its taste is a bit _____.

9. Many see picking one's nose in public as a(n) _____ habit.

10. If you _____ these ideas from your paper, the strength of your thesis will be greatly diminished.

NEW WORDS

wither
ˈwiTHər

entertain
ˌentərˈtān

indulgent
inˈdəljənt

instance
ˈinstəns

zenith
ˈzēniTH

Jack and Jill went to a remote mountain resort to witness the **zenith** of the North Star away from city lights. No one could possibly accuse this young couple of being **indulgent** with their money. Their luxury trip epitomizes an **instance** when ambitious, hard working recent college graduates chose not to let their passion for astronomy **wither** soon after graduation. On the contrary, they chose to **entertain** no thought of giving up on their sky gazing passion. Instead, they rather took it to new heights. Literally.

Definitions: Try matching the words in the list with the appropriate definitions. If you are stuck, check the glossary in the back of the book or the passage at the top of the page.

1.	wither	_____	a.	the highest point reached by a celestial or other object
2.	entertain	_____	b.	1. to provide someone with amusement or enjoyment; 2. to give attention or consideration to an idea, suggestion, or feeling
3.	indulgent	_____	c.	having or indicating a tendency to be overly generous or lenient with someone
4.	instance	_____	d.	(of a plant) to become dry and shriveled; (of a person) to become shrunken or wrinkled from age or disease; to cease to flourish
5.	zenith	_____	e.	an example or single occurrence of something

Sentences: Try to use the words above in a sentence below. Remember that a word ending may be changed or its figure of speech slightly altered.

6.   It appears that the sun is at its _____ at high noon.

7.   Comedies are meant to _____ their viewers, for it is important to laugh in life.

8.   Uncle Morris is really _____: every time I come in town to visit him, he takes me to all of my favorite candy stores and shopping malls.

9.   After several days of not watering my yucca plant, its leaves began to _____.

10.   I cannot think of a single _____ when my mother failed to be responsible as a parent.

Lesson 66

THE ELDER FROM THE MOUNTAINS

The old man had a **luminous** presence: he seemed so joyful and light, almost out of this world. Many people came to the monastery to see him. He was **hospitable** and gave everyone his attention. His presence seemed to **encompass** everything and everyone. Even though big crowds of people came to visit him from all over the world, there was nothing **pretentious** about him. He remained humble and lived in the same small room with **scant** belongings: just a small bed, a blanket, and a few pieces of clothing.

Definitions: Try matching the words in the list with the appropriate definitions. If you are stuck, check the glossary in the back of the book or the passage at the top of the page.

1.	luminous _____	a.	friendly and welcoming to guests; (of an environment) pleasant and favorable for living in	
2.	hospitable _____	b.	attempting to impress by assuming greater importance, talent, culture, or credibility than one actually possesses	
3.	encompass _____	c.	small or insufficient in quantity or amount	
4.	scant _____	d.	to surround or enclose within; to include comprehensively	
5.	pretentious _____	e.	full of light; shedding light; bright or shining, especially in the dark	

Sentences: Try to use the words above in a sentence below. Remember that a word ending may be changed or its figure of speech slightly altered.

6.   Usually in the spring when the snow melts and the storms subside, New England's weather becomes increasingly _____.

7.   Topics to be discussed at the policy brunch this week _____ a variety of humanitarian issues ranging from child trafficking problems to nutrition and gender equality.

8.   My neighbor praised the new pub for its generous portions, but I found my meal there to be quite _____.

9.   At deep depths in the ocean there can be found many _____ animals brightening the waters proximate to them.

10.   The _____ vixen sauntered into the room as if she owned the venue.

NEW WORDS

progressive
prə'gresiv

prudish
'proŏdiSH

dissonance
'disənəns

sanitary
'saniˌterē

replica
'replikə

SCHOOL CHANGES

The new school principal hoped to make his institution a much more **progressive** place. Among the changes he wanted to implement was to let students wear clothing of their choice in lieu of school uniforms. Yet pushing to change this policy stirred up **dissonance** between the school's **prudish**, conservative faculty and its newer liberal teachers. The principal also wanted to turn the squalid school cafeteria into a viable study space in late afternoons. He presented a **replica** of the local community college cafeteria space at the last faculty meeting to serve as a model for his vision. Implementing such changes, he asserted, would create not only a better educational environment, but also a more **sanitary** one.

Definitions: Try matching the words in the list with the appropriate definitions. If you are stuck, check the glossary in the back of the book or the passage at the top of the page.

1. progressive _____   a. of or relating to conditions affecting health or hygiene
2. prudish _____   b. having the tendency to be easily shocked by matters related to sex or nudity
3. dissonance _____   c. lack of harmony between two or more musical notes; a tension resulting from a combination of two or more unsuitable elements
4. sanitary _____   d. an exact copy or model of something, often on a smaller scale
5. replica _____   e. 1. developing in stages; proceeding step by step; 2. favoring or implementing social reform or new, liberal ideas

Sentences: Try to use the words above in a sentence below. Remember that a word ending may be changed or its figure of speech slightly altered.

6. Ideas such as homosexual marriage were considered to be _____ in the 1960s.
7. The _____ between the two professors only grew worse after one claimed that the other's work was plagiarized.
8. If restaurants do not keep their kitchens in _____ condition, the Board of Health may come and shut them down.
9. My aunt has such a(n) _____ attitude: she yelled at me because I was reading a fashion magazine with some provocative photos in it.
10. The Queens Museum has a famous _____ of Manhattan on display.

Lesson 68

BLIND BELIEF

A **preponderance** of people in the kingdom believed that the origins of the new king were **sacred**. After all, the head priest had convinced them that the new king was a divine man. The people had no doubt that the newcomer would **accede** to their requests that he assume the throne. Just the sight of his glamorous attire and his golden scepter would **stupefy** them. They believed that the new king could **evoke** myriad divine powers with his golden scepter and were mortally afraid of him.

NEW WORDS

sacred
ˈsākrid

preponderance
priˈpändərəns

accede
akˈsēd

evoke
iˈvōk

stupefy
ˈst(y)o͞opəˌfī

Definitions: Try matching the words in the list with the appropriate definitions. If you are stuck, check the glossary in the back of the book or the passage at the top of the page.

1.	sacred _____	a.	to assent or agree to a request, demand, or treaty
2.	preponderance _____	b.	1. religious rather than secular; 2. something connected with God or the gods and thus worthy of veneration; 3. regarded with great reverence and respect
3.	accede _____	c.	the fact or quality of being great in number, quantity, extent, or importance
4.	evoke _____	d.	to bring or call to mind; to elicit a response; to invoke a spirit or deity
5.	stupefy _____	e.	to astonish and shock, often to the point of being unable to think or act properly

Sentences: Try to use the words above in a sentence below. Remember that a word ending may be changed or its figure of speech slightly altered.

6. The Torah is considered to be a(n) _____ object in the Jewish tradition.

7. It was difficult to get my parents to _____ to my arrangement to spend spring break in the Bahamas.

8. The eerie music at the beginning of the play _____ a sense of fright that is intended to last throughout the performance.

9. Albert noted that there was a(n) _____ of sugar in his aunt's cake; it tasted far too sweet for his liking.

10. Harris was _____ when he heard that his sister's boyfriend was a prince.

Lesson 69

THE REBEL

NEW WORDS

process
'prä͵ses, 'präsəs, 'prō-

contempt
kən'tem(p)t

eminent
'emənənt

mischief
'misCHif

stolid
'stälid

During the legal **process**, Jason had a **stolid** expression in his face, as if nothing mattered to him. He knew that painting the teacher's car was not merely **mischief** and that he had to face the consequences. At the same time, he was barely trying to hide his **contempt** for both the legal system and for the teacher. An **eminent** prankster at his school, Jason was known for his disdain for authority and for his rebellious views about social systems.

Definitions: Try matching the words in the list with the appropriate definitions. If you are stuck, check the glossary in the back of the book or the passage at the top of the page.

1.   process   _____   a.   1. a feeling that a person is beneath consideration, deserving scorn, or unworthy; 2. a disregard for something that should be taken into account

2.   contempt   _____   b.   characterizing one who is calm and showing little emotion

3.   eminent   _____   c.   (n.) series of actions or steps taken in order to achieve a particular end; (v.) to perform a series of mechanical or chemical operations on something in order to change or preserve it

4.   mischief   _____   d.   playful behavior often involved in troublemaking and usually exhibited by children; playfulness intended to tease, mock, and create trouble; harm or trouble caused by something

5.   stolid   _____   e.   characterizing a person who is famous or respected within a certain field or profession

Sentences: Try to use the words above in a sentence below. Remember that a word ending may be changed or its figure of speech slightly altered.

6.   René Descartes (1596-1650) is heralded by scholars as a(n) _____ mathematician in early modern Europe.

7.   The child got into _____ to see how far he could push social norms.

8.   I have nothing but _____ for the people who stole my computer.

9.   Grief is a(n) _____: it takes time to make peace with another's passing.

10.   Dave is a(n) _____ man who did not even cry at his father's funeral.

Lesson 70

STAYING TRUE TO YOURSELF

After the **massive** success of his book, the writer was approached by **inquisitive** television producers. They asked him a **variety** of questions, but their main concern was whether he would be willing to turn the book into a movie. They wanted to know if he would **tailor** the plot to a sensation-hungry audience and change some aspects of the original story. The writer agreed to do so, but only if the television producers left him $500,000 as **collateral** for his intellectual property. The writer, however, ultimately declined their offers and declared his intention to stay true to the original narrative.

NEW WORDS

massive
ˈmasiv

inquisitive
inˈkwizitiv, iNG-

collateral
kəˈlatərəl, kəˈlatrəl

tailor
ˈtālər

variety
vəˈrīətē

Definitions: Try matching the words in the list with the appropriate definitions. If you are stuck, check the glossary in the back of the book or the passage at the top of the page.

1. massive _____
2. inquisitive _____
3. collateral _____
4. tailor _____
5. variety _____

a. something pledged as security for repayment of a loan
b. (n.) a person whose occupation is to adjust clothing (suits, pants, jackets) to fit individual customers; (v.) 1. to make clothes fit individual customers; 2. to make or adapt for a particular purpose or person
c. the quality of being different or diverse; the absence of sameness; lacking homogeneity
d. curious and asking many questions
e. exceptionally large, heavy, solid, or important

Sentences: Try to use the words above in a sentence below. Remember that a word ending may be changed or its figure of speech slightly altered.

6. Because Peter did not have money to pay his mortgage last month, he offered his landlord his designer watch as _____.
7. It is important to have a good _____ to adjust your pants; if you don't they will not fit you well.
8. The moon is a(n) _____ body that orbits the earth.
9. There are a(n) _____ of reasons why I do not like my stepmother: she is cruel, she does not speak to me, and she does not value education.
10. Many scientists believe that macaque monkeys are exceptionally intelligent because of their _____ nature.

Word Search

Lessons 61-70

```
P E N E C N A T S N I F O S T E R
R V Q O H S I D U R P V E G X N Y
E I E V I T I S I U Q N I B T M J
S S S L K S V P E J T B O N R M D
U S U C B L S K E E M I G N J X V
M E O O Q A O A R S S N G D Y N N
P R N N D V T T P T T I R R D R R
T G I T E I A I E M E E T P R P
U O M E A I L R P R O B R S T T M
O R U M N I O O E S M C A Z R R T
U P L P H U L V T O O C D K J W P
S Y W T S K O O S S R H N L R G T
Q Z A T L S M K R E Z J L Z V M M
M O N P R V W T D T M Y P Y B Q J
```

1 (adj.) dark or dull in color and tone; gloomy
2 (n.) a solemn promise, often invoking a divine witness, regarding one's future behavior or action
3 (v.) to encourage or promote the development of something; to develop a feeling or idea within oneself
4 (adj.) (concerning a person and his or her behavior) failing to observe the limits of what is deemed appropriate
5 (adj.) possessing supreme or ultimate power; (n.) a supreme ruler, especially a monarch
6 (v.) to trouble or annoy someone with frequent interruptions or requests
7 (adj.) 1. (of a person, event, or occasion) energetic, noisy, and cheerful; 2. (of wind, weather, or water) wild or stormy
8 (n.) sympathetic pity and concern for the suffering and misfortunes of others
9 (v.) 1. to provide someone with amusement or enjoyment; 2. to give attention or consideration to an idea, suggestion, or feeling
10 (n.) an example or single occurrence of something
11 (adj.) full of light; shedding light; bright or shining, especially in the dark
12 (adj.) friendly and welcoming to guests; (of an environment) pleasant and favorable for living in
13 (adj.) 1. developing in stages; proceeding step by step; 2. favoring or implementing social reform or new, liberal ideas
14 (adj.) having the tendency to be easily shocked by matters related to sex or nudity
15 (adj.) 1. religious rather than secular; 2. something connected with God or the gods and thus worthy of veneration; 3. regarded with great reverence and respect
16 (v.) to bring or call to mind; to elicit a response; to invoke a spirit or deity
17 (n.) 1. a feeling that a person is beneath consideration, deserving scorn, or unworthy; 2. a disregard for something that should be taken into account
18 (adj.) characterizing one who is calm, dependable and showing little emotion
19 (adj.) curious and asking many questions
20 (n.) a person whose occupation is to adjust clothing (suits, pants, jackets) to fit individual customers; (v.) 1. to make clothes fit individual customers; 2. to make or adapt for a particular purpose or person

Vocabulary Review
Lessons 61-70

Directions: Match each word with its best approximate definition. Note that definitions are not necessarily repeated verbatim from the lesson exercises.

1. tardy   _____
2. cultivate   _____
3. furious   _____
4. brazen   _____
5. pariah   _____
6. ensnare   _____
7. acrid   _____
8. repugnant   _____
9. indulgent   _____
10. zenith   _____
11. encompass   _____
12. scant   _____
13. sanitary   _____
14. replica   _____
15. preponderance   _____
16. accede   _____
17. eminent   _____
18. mischief   _____
19. massive   _____
20. collateral   _____

a. concerning conditions related to health or hygiene
b. an outcast
c. extremely angry
d. small or insufficient quantity
e. to surround and enclose within; to include comprehensively
f. playful misbehavior or troublemaking, often from children
g. catch in or as in a trap
h. to raise or grow (especially plants); to acquire and develop
i. to assent or agree to a demand, request, or treaty
j. having a bitter or unpleasant taste or smell
k. bold and without shame
l. extremely distasteful; unacceptable
m. being great in quality, number, or importance
n. exceptionally large and heavy or solid
o. the highest point reached by a celestial or other object
p. having a tendency to be too generous with someone
q. a person who is famous and respected within his or her profession
r. something pledged as repayment for a loan, to be forfeited in case of default
s. delaying or being delayed beyond the expected time
t. an exact copy or model of something, often on a smaller scale

Word Roots: Unit 7

ROOTS AND THEIR MEANINGS

neo/nov:	new	derm:	skin
carn:	flesh	equ(i):	equal
extra:	beyond, outside	anti:	against, opposite

Here are a few examples of some words that use the above roots:

neophyte:	a novice, a beginner
carnage:	the killing of a large number of people
extraterrestrial:	from beyond the earth or its atmosphere
dermatologist:	a doctor who diagnoses and treats skin disorders
equivalent:	equal in value, amount, or function
antisocial:	not wanting the company of other people

Now try to fill in the table below by finding the appropriate root(s) and interpreting the meaning of each word:

Word	Root(s)	Guessed Meaning	Actual Meaning
equanimity			
carnal			
extraordinary			
equivocate			
reincarnation			
dermal			
antithetical			
extravagant			
novice			
antithesis			
innovate			

Lesson 71

THE NIGHT BEFORE THE BATTLE

The knights visited a **seer**, hoping that she would be able to foretell the future of the battle. They were **incredulous** by nature, however, the fear of the impending fight made them less skeptical. The seer stared into her magic ball and told them that they needed to first attack the **sentry** at the castle gate. At the same time, she seemed to **insinuate** that the knights would lose the battle. Driven by anger, the knights told the seer that her vision was **preposterous** and that they would win the fight under all circumstances.

Definitions: Try matching the words in the list with the appropriate definitions. If you are stuck, check the glossary in the back of the book or the passage at the top of the page.

1.	preposterous _____	a.	absurd or ridiculous; contrary to common sense
2.	insinuate _____	b.	a person who is able to see what the future holds
3.	sentry _____	c.	to suggest or hint at (something bad or reprehensible) in an unpleasant way
4.	incredulous _____	d.	a soldier stationed to keep guard over a place
5.	seer _____	e.	a person who is unable or unwilling to believe something

Sentences: Try to use the words above in a sentence below. Remember that a word ending may be changed or its figure of speech slightly altered.

6.   It is _____ to believe that someone with no knowledge of a foreign language could become fluent in that language in one day.

7.   Two _____ guarded the gate to the palace that I hoped to pass through.

8.   Ingrid was _____ when she saw that she had failed all of her midterm exams.

9.   Willy's boss tried to _____ that his colleagues did not respect him, but such communication fell on deaf ears.

10.   Only a(n) _____ can know for sure whether I will live to be one hundred years old.

NEW WORDS

expenditure
ikˈspendiCHər

smite
smīt

onus
ˈōnəs

statute
ˈstaCHoōt

chaff
CHaf

DRAMA AT WORK

A key **statute** of the organization prohibited many of Michael's business expenses. About half of his business **expenditure** covered lavish personal hotel and phone bills. When confronted by the board of directors about this matter, Michael tried to place the **onus** of the blame on his personal assistant, who he claimed was not a responsible person. Such accusations would **smite** the assistant's reputation. Ultimately the assistant was terminated, likely because Michael was regarded as an honest, responsible worker. In fact, many of his co-workers liked to **chaff** him for staying at work late. Thus, the assistant felt that his boss blamed him unjustly for his own carelessness.

Definitions: Try matching the words in the list with the appropriate definitions. If you are stuck, check the glossary in the back of the book or the passage at the top of the page.

1. expenditure _____ a. a written law passed by a legislative body; a rule of an organization or institution
2. smite _____ b. (n.) a heavy blow with a weapon or from the hand; (v.) 1. to strike with a firm blow; 2. to affect severely
3. onus _____ c. the action of spending funds
4. statute _____ d. used to refer to something that is one's duty or responsibility
5. chaff _____ e. to tease

Sentences: Try to use the words above in a sentence below. Remember that a word ending may be changed or its figure of speech slightly altered.

6. Most people's basic monthly _____ are on rent and food.
7. The boys joked and _____ with each other about my asking a supermodel on a date.
8. The leader of the rebel army prayed to the gods that divine intervention would _____ their enemies.
9. Often parents bear the _____ of accountability for their children's behavior.
10. In early 2015, Congress was looking to repeal a(n) _____ declaring it illegal to curse in front of women and children.

Lesson 73

THE OLD SAGE

Everyone revered the old **sage**. His reputation was **untainted**, as his actions were always regarded as noble and unassuming. Often the look in his eyes would **express** boundless compassion for all beings. He also seemed to possess much **brawn** despite his incredibly advanced age. His name had a positive **connotation** in everyone's recollection: all of the town folk admired him and looked up to him.

Definitions: Try matching the words in the list with the appropriate definitions. If you are stuck, check the glossary in the back of the book or the passage at the top of the page.

1. express _____ a. (adj.) operating at high speed; (n.) a rapid moving vehicle or delivery service; (v.) 1. to convey a thought or feeling in words or by gestures and conduct; 2. to send quickly or at high speed

2. brawn _____ b. (adj.) wise; (n.) a profoundly wise (and often old) person

3. connotation_____ c. physical strength (in contrast to intelligence)

4. sage _____ d. an idea or feeling that a word evokes in addition to its literal meaning

5. untainted _____ e. not contaminated or polluted

Sentences: Try to use the words above in a sentence below. Remember that a word ending may be changed or its figure of speech slightly altered.

6. It is important to _____ one's feelings eloquently and clearly so that others can comprehend them.

7. Shayna may be the brains behind the operation, but it would not succeed without Douglas' _____ and sheer power.

8. The word "lazy" generally bears a negative _____ because it is associated with a lack of desire to do anything, which is not perceived as positive.

9. Often grandparents are good sources for _____ advice: having lived for quite some time, they know best about how to handle many circumstances.

10. Because of its distance from the metropolis, rural Clarkville remained largely _____ by air pollution and toxins produced in the big city.

NEW WORDS

nutritious
n(y)oo̅ˈtriSHəs

brash
braSH

forestall
fôrˈstôl

diminish
diˈminiSH

phobia
ˈfōbēə

DEATH IN THE FAMILY

Martin's fear of leaving the house after his mother's death turned into a **phobia**. He would sit in his room and rely on his older sister, Amy, for food. Amy tried to alleviate his fears and brought him **nutritious** meals in order to keep him healthy. Despite Amy's help, sometimes Martin made **brash** and rude remarks toward her. He was scared and angry at the whole world. Amy felt that her efforts to help him could not **forestall** his anger. However, Martin's hostility did not **diminish** her resolution to help him overcome their mother's death.

Definitions: Try matching the words in the list with the appropriate definitions. If you are stuck, check the glossary in the back of the book or the passage at the top of the page.

1. nutritious _____
2. brash _____
3. forestall _____
4. diminish _____
5. phobia _____

a. to prevent an event or action from happening by taking advance action; an act to delay
b. an extreme or irrational fear of or aversion to something
c. to make or become less
d. self-assertive in a rude, overbearing, or noisy way; overbearing
e. nourishing and efficient as food

Sentences: Try to use the words above in a sentence below. Remember that a word ending may be changed or its figure of speech slightly altered.

6. Fruits and vegetables are _____ snacks, for they contain many vitamins that are good for one's health.

7. Feelings of sadness in grieving the loss of a loved one will eventually _____ in time.

8. Unlike her urbane aunt, Nicoletta is _____ and voices her opinion on many matters boldly and self-confidently.

9. Hannah has many _____: she is afraid of cockroaches, the number thirteen, and black cats.

10. The students tried to _____ their math quiz by bombarding their teacher with questions during the entire class period.

Lesson 75

A HAPLESS STATE

The **portentous** fire burned down the only hospital in the region and chaos soon ensued. Without medical equipment and facilities, people who were injured during the fire – covered in burns, wounds, and **char** marks – were left untreated for weeks. With the unstable political climate of the country and a lack of infrastructure, it was impossible for international organizations to **donate** resources in a timely manner; as a result, the injured did not receive **equitable** treatment. The **inextricable** link between poverty and disease had never been more evident.

Definitions: Try matching the words in the list with the appropriate definitions. If you are stuck, check the glossary in the back of the book or the passage at the top of the page.

1.	donate	_____	a.	fair and impartial
2.	char	_____	b.	impossible to disentangle or separate; impossible to escape from
3.	inextricable	_____	c.	ominously significant or important; momentous
4.	equitable	_____	d.	to partially burn an object as to blacken its surface
5.	portentous	_____	e.	1. to give one's money or goods for a cause, especially a charity; 2. to allow the removal of one's blood or organ(s) from one's body for transplant or transfusion

Sentences: Try to use the words above in a sentence below. Remember that a word ending may be changed or its figure of speech slightly altered.

6.   After the dispute, the magistrate hoped to find a(n) _____ solution that could satisfy both parties.

7.   How _____ it was when dark clouds swirled above the battleground in the hours before the slaughter.

8.   It seems that the chef _____ my lunch: my chicken breast is partially black and flaking apart.

9.   Every year my family _____ clothing and canned soup to help the homeless.

10.   For many physicists, the concept of relativity is _____ linked to that of the Bohr model of the atom.

NEW WORDS

enormous
iˈnôrməs

prestidigitation
ˌprestəˌdijəˈtāSHən

appropriate
əˈprōprē-it (adj.); -ˌāt (v.)

negligent
ˈnegləjənt

populate
ˈpäpyəˌlāt

CORRUPT OFFICIAL

Despite the fact that Ricky was a **negligent** official who preferred sitting on the veranda and smoking cigars to doing his work, he exerted **enormous** power in the small colonial community. Through remarkable **prestidigitation**, he was able to replace genuine business contracts filed at the county office with counterfeit ones, thus enabling him to control many of the local establishments and **appropriate** the largest part of their profits. His power seemed to be boundless. However, as more educated families began to **populate** the area, Ricky found that he could no longer maintain his position through deception and dangerous charisma.

Definitions: Try matching the words in the list with the appropriate definitions. If you are stuck, check the glossary in the back of the book or the passage at the top of the page.

1.   enormous _____   a.   to fill with people; to form the population of a particular town, area, or country
2.   prestidigitation _____   b.   slight of hand; legerdemain
3.   appropriate_____   c.   very large in size, quantity, or extent
4.   negligent _____   d.   failing to take proper care in doing something
5.   populate _____   e.   (adj.) suitable or proper in the circumstances; (v.) 1. to take something for one's use, typically without permission; 2. to devote money or assets to a special purpose

Sentences: Try to use the words above in a sentence below. Remember that a word ending may be changed or its figure of speech slightly altered.

6.   Because Rochelle was _____, he cousin crawled onto a hot stove and burnt his hand.
7.   Over 300,000 people _____ the state of California in the years 1848-55 after James W. Marshall discovered gold at Sutter's Mill in Coloma.
8.   With careful _____, the magician made the coin disappear right before my eyes.
9.   The new house being built at the cul-de-sac is _____: it appears to have at least a dozen bedrooms!
10.   It is not _____ to wear a swimsuit and lei to an American funeral.

Lesson 77

YOU REAP WHAT YOU SOW

The newspaper was full of misinformation and **propaganda**. Journalists had the liberty to **concoct** any story they wished, as long as it reflected the paper's ideology. One day, someone threatened to sue the newspaper based on the **fallacy** of the information that the paper printed. The newspaper office suddenly became so quiet that one could hear the **somnolent** hum of grasshoppers outside. Eventually, the court issued a **requisition** to the newspaper for the payment of $10,000 to the plaintiff.

Definitions: Try matching the words in the list with the appropriate definitions. If you are stuck, check the glossary in the back of the book or the passage at the top of the page.

1. propaganda _____   a. a mistaken belief, especially one founded on unsound argument

2. concoct _____   b. sleepy or drowsy

3. somnolent _____   c. (n.) an official order laying claim to the use of property or materials; (v.) to demand the use or supply of, especially by official order and for military or public use

4. fallacy _____   d. 1. to make a dish or meal by combining various ingredients; 2. to create or devise a story or plan

5. requisition _____   e. information that is typically biased or misleading that is used to promote or publicize a particular political cause or point of view

Sentences: Try to use the words above in a sentence below. Remember that a word ending may be changed or its figure of speech slightly altered.

6. The library has obtained permission to _____ three paintings from the local art gallery.

7. Often governments will use _____ to get others to believe their creed.

8. It is a(n) _____ to believe everything that the media says: even news companies have their own biases in outlook and hires.

9. My _____ boss kept dozing off at work this morning; I'm not sure if he slept last night!

10. Lydia _____ a story about why she did not show up at work yesterday; sadly, I'm not sure that anyone believed it.

NEW WORDS

dormant
ˈdôrmənt

ideal
īˈdē(ə)l

exist
igˈzist

scathing
ˈskāT͟HiNG

unswerving
ˌənˈswərviNG

THE AWAKENING

A sense of social justice was **dormant** in Jerome for many years. He knew he was treated unfairly at work, but he needed the money to feed his family. Long ago, as a child, Jerome had believed in an **ideal** world – a society in which everyone was equal. After so many years, during a company meeting, the **scathing** remarks of his boss finally woke Jerome up. Jerome was surprised to see that dignity and self-respect could still **exist** in him. Feeling humiliated by his boss, he immediately left his job. For the first time in his adult life, Jerome was filled with an **unswerving** commitment to follow his own sense of justice.

Definitions: Try matching the words in the list with the appropriate definitions. If you are stuck, check the glossary in the back of the book or the passage at the top of the page.

1.	dormant	_____	a.	steady or constant; unchanging or unwavering
2.	ideal	_____	b.	severely critical or scornful
3.	exist	_____	c.	1. to have objective reality or being; 2. to live (under especially adverse conditions)
4.	scathing	_____	d.	1. (of an animal) having normal physical functions suspended as if in a deep sleep; 2. (of a volcano) temporarily inactive; 3. (of a disease) showing no symptoms but liable to recur
5.	unswerving	_____	e.	(adj.) satisfying one's conception of what is perfect or most suitable; (n.) a person or thing regarded as perfect; a standard of perfection or principle to be aimed at

Sentences: Try to use the words above in a sentence below. Remember that a word ending may be changed or its figure of speech slightly altered.

6.   The volcano on that island has been _____ for nearly four decades.

7.   My _____ girlfriend would be attractive, honest, communicative, altruistic, and dedicated to her work.

8.   Though rare, it is true that four-leaf clovers do _____: perhaps one in every 10,000 clovers has four leaves.

9.   The senator's _____ remarks left his government colleagues speechless and offended.

10.   Sasha's _____ commitment to her studies should help her earn a spot at a top university.

Lesson 79

WITH BATED BREATH

As soon as the news broke that James would not follow into the family **tradition** of becoming a perfume creator, members of his family wondered what had **transpired** that caused him to make this decision. Indeed, hey waited with bated breath to hear about James' career choice. They were **ravenous** to know what new use James's impeccable **olfactory** senses would be put to. Knowing what a rare and nuanced sense of smell James has, I would not put it past his family to **connive** a plan that forces James to reconsider his career options in favor of his good old perfume designer destiny.

Definitions: Try matching the words in the list with the appropriate definitions. If you are stuck, check the glossary in the back of the book or the passage at the top of the page.

1.	transpire	_____	a.	to occur or happen
2.	tradition	_____	b.	extremely hungry
3.	ravenous	_____	c.	the transmission of customs and beliefs from one generation to the next
4.	connive	_____	d.	of or relating to the sense of smell
5.	olfactory	_____	e.	to secretly allow something immoral, illegal, wrong, or harmful to occur (often conspiring with others)

Sentences: Try to use the words above in a sentence below. Remember that a word ending may be changed or its figure of speech slightly altered.

6.   When one has a common cold, _____ senses may be suppressed.

7.   I do not know what _____ when I was on vacation last week; that is why I'm asking my assistant to fill me in on the details of all transactions.

8.   The dog was so _____ that he devoured food as soon as it was set out for him.

9.   Out of spite, the employees are _____ to get their boss fired.

10.   It is a family _____ to go to the beach on Independence Day.

NEW WORDS

shun
SHən

null
nəl

malicious
məˈliSHəs

ransack
ˈranˌsak, ranˈsak

adept
əˈdept

PAINFUL MEMORIES

The marriage was now **null** and void, and Deborah tried to **shun** any attempt on Tom's part to visit the apartment and retrieve his belongings. Deborah had always been **adept** at avoiding unpleasant situations. It was not that she was purposefully **malicious** and wanted to deprive Tom of things that held sentimental value for him. She simply could not bear to see Tom **ransack** their old home looking for memories. She knew this would be too painful for her.

Definitions: Try matching the words in the list with the appropriate definitions. If you are stuck, check the glossary in the back of the book or the passage at the top of the page.

1. shun _____ a. to persistently avoid, ignore, or reject someone or something through antipathy or caution

2. null _____ b. characterized by an intention to do harm

3. malicious _____ c. to move hurriedly through a place stealing things and causing damage

4. ransack _____ d. very skilled or proficient at something

5. adept _____ e. 1. having no legal or binding force; invalid; 2. having or associated with the value zero

Sentences: Try to use the words above in a sentence below. Remember that a word ending may be changed or its figure of speech slightly altered.

6. Jill _____ her ex-boyfriend's attempt to try and rebuild their relationship.

7. In some societies' history, marriage between people of two different races was deemed to be _____.

8. One has to be _____ with numbers if he or she desires an actuarial career.

9. The unruly children _____ the doctor's home on Halloween, destroying her mailbox and stealing all of her holiday candy.

10. Only a(n) _____ person would try to sabotage another person's career for fun.

Crossword Puzzle
Lessons 71-80

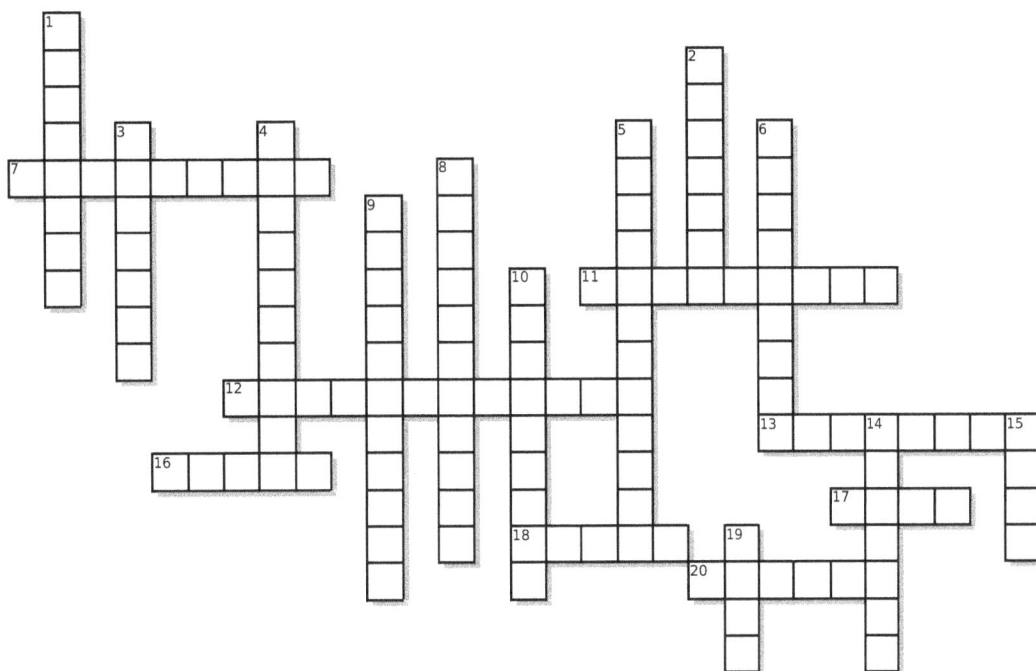

ACROSS

7 (adj.) of or relating to the sense of smell
11 (v.) to prevent an event or action from happening by taking advance action; to delay
12 (adj.) impossible to disentangle or separate; impossible to escape from
13 (adj.) very large in size, quantity, or extent
16 (adj.) satisfying one's conception of what is perfect or most suitable; (n.) a person or thing regarded as perfect; a standard of perfection or principle to be aimed at
17 (n.) used to refer to something that is one's duty or responsibility
18 (v.) 1. to have objective reality or being; 2. to live under adverse conditions
20 (n.) an extreme or irrational fear of or aversion to something

DOWN

1 (v.) to fill with people; to form the population of a particular town, area, or country
2 (v.) to secretly allow something immoral, illegal, wrong, or harmful to occur
3 (n.) a mistaken belief, especially one founded on unsound argument
4 (n.) information that is typically biased or misleading that is used to promote or publicize a particular political cause or point of view
5 (adj.) absurd or ridiculous; contrary to common sense
6 (adj.) fair and impartial
8 (n.) the action of spending funds
9 (n.) an idea or feeling that a word evokes in addition to its literal meaning
10 (adj.) not contaminated or polluted
14 (v.) to move hurriedly through a place stealing things and causing damage
15 (n.) a person who is able to see what the future holds
19 (v.) to persistently avoid, ignore, or reject someone or something through antipathy or caution

Vocabulary Review
Lessons 71-80

Directions: Match each word with its best approximate definition. Note that definitions are not necessarily repeated verbatim from the lesson exercises.

1.	sentry	_____	a.	physical strength in contrast to intelligence
2.	incredulous	_____	b.	concerning a warning that something bad is likely to happen
3.	statute	_____	c.	steady, constant; steadfast
4.	chaff	_____	d.	to occur or happen
5.	brawn	_____	e.	failing to take proper care in doing something
6.	sage	_____	f.	sleight of hand
7.	nutritious	_____	g.	a soldier stationed to keep guard or to control access to a place
8.	diminish	_____	h.	characterized by an intention to do harm
9.	char	_____	i.	very skilled or proficient at something
10.	portentous	_____	j.	sleepy or drowsy
11.	prestidigitation	_____	k.	to make or become less
12.	negligent	_____	l.	extremely critical or scornful
13.	concoct	_____	m.	lighthearted joking or banter
14.	somnolent	_____	n.	a written law that is passed by a legislative body
15.	scathing	_____	o.	to partially burn an object or to blacken its surface
16.	unswerving	_____	p.	extremely hungry
17.	transpire	_____	q.	unwilling or unable to believe something
18.	ravenous	_____	r.	to make up something (a dish, meal, or lie) by combining various ingredients
19.	malicious	_____	s.	something that is efficient as food; nourishing
20.	adept	_____	t.	showing wisdom; a profoundly wise man

Word Roots: Unit 8

ROOTS AND THEIR MEANINGS

dign/dian:	**worth (value)**	**in/en/em/im:**	**into**
nai/nas/nat:	**to be born**	**phon:**	**sound**
gen:	**type, birth**	**fac:**	**to do; to make**
ad/at:	**to, toward**	**cli:**	**to lean**

Here are a few examples of some words that use the above roots:

dignity:	the state of equality in being worthy of honor or respect
renaissance:	the rebirth of something, usually art or music
genotype:	the genetic composition of an organism
advance:	to move forward or make progress, typically with an expressed purpose
immerse:	to submerge in a liquid
incarnate:	embodied in human form or in the flesh
telephone:	an instrument by which one can communicate with others at a distance
facilitate:	to make a process or an action easier
inclination:	a natural tendency to act or behave in a certain way

Now try to fill in the table below by finding the appropriate root(s) and interpreting the meaning of each word:

Word	Root(s)	Guessed Meaning	Actual Meaning
factory			
phonetics			
nationality			
proclivity			
nascence			
attain			
genealogy			
engaged			
generic			
engrossing			
decline			

NEW WORDS

felon
ˈfelən

exotic
igˈzätik

stifle
ˈstīfəl

provocative
prəˈväkətiv

benefactor
ˈbenəˌfaktər, ˌbenəˈfaktər

The **felon**, Mr. Joyce, had to **stifle** his anger in the court. He knew that if he became enraged in front of the judge, his penalty would become even more severe. As far as he was concerned, the victim – a young native boy – had acted in an emotionally **provocative** manner with his **exotic** story about his unhappy childhood and gang history. The boy had made Mr. Joyce feel like his **benefactor**. Thus, when the boy ran away with Mr. Joyce's money, it seemed justified that Mr. Joyce would chase him down and try to seek revenge.

Definitions: Try matching the words in the list with the appropriate definitions. If you are stuck, check the glossary in the back of the book or the passage at the top of the page.

1. felon _____ a. to suffocate; to stop one from acting on an emotion; to restrain or prevent
2. exotic _____ b. deliberately evoking annoyance, anger, or another strong reaction; deliberately attempting to arouse sexual desire
3. stifle _____ c. a person who gives money or other aid to a person or cause
4. provocative_____ d. originating in or characteristic of a foreign country; appealing because of having come from a far away place
5. benefactor _____ e. a person who has been convicted of a felony

Sentences: Try to use the words above in a sentence below. Remember that a word ending may be changed or its figure of speech slightly altered.

6. Maria did not realize that she was _____ her students' interest in mathematics by refusing to answer more advanced questions than what the textbook taught.
7. The only reason an actress would wear a(n) _____ outfit like that is to get the attention of the media or of some man.
8. For most Americans, _____ birds are fascinating because local varieties neither have brightly colored plumage nor can squawk out words.
9. As one of the _____ of the school, I strongly believe in helping people develop the ability to help themselves learn.
10. The _____ escaped from jail in the middle of the night and was unable to be apprehended by authorities.

Lesson 82

A LIFE CRISIS

It seemed that nothing could **impede** Bob's oncoming existential crisis. No matter how much he tried to **refrain** from thinking, Bob could not forget that in just a few days his superiors would **demote** him to the lower rank of a junior officer. His future now seemed like an open **abyss**: it seemed that if he looked down, he would drown. It was not until many months later that Bob was able to forgive himself for his misdeed and take **tentative** steps back to positivity and self-belief.

NEW WORDS

impede
imˈpēd

refrain
riˈfrān

demote
diˈmōt

abyss
əˈbis

tentative
ˈtentətiv

Definitions: Try matching the words in the list with the appropriate definitions. If you are stuck, check the glossary in the back of the book or the passage at the top of the page.

1.	impede	_____	a.	to stop oneself from doing something
2.	refrain	_____	b.	not certain or fixed; provisional
3.	demote	_____	c.	to give someone a lower rank or less senior position, usually as a punishment
4.	abyss	_____	d.	to delay or prevent someone or something by preventing him, her, or it
5.	tentative	_____	e.	a deep or seemingly bottomless chasm

Sentences: Try to use the words above in a sentence below. Remember that a word ending may be changed or its figure of speech slightly altered.

6. It is important to _____ from talking during a movie.

7. Though a difficult decision to make, the company decided to _____ three of its managers because they were not performing up to par.

8. It seems that almost nothing can _____ the growth of the city; prices are cheap, jobs are abundant, and there is much to do downtown.

9. That canyon is so deep that it feels like a(n) _____.

10. I have _____ plans to go to the zoo on Friday to draw animals, but if need be I could alter those arrangements.

NEW WORDS

confusion
kən'fyooZHən

genteel
jen'tēl

prediction
pri'dikSHən

annex
ə'neks, 'aneks

falsetto
fôl'setō

TROUBLES IN THE COMPANY

Whenever Philip got angry, he sang in an unusually high, unpleasant **falsetto**. Philip was a man of **genteel** upbringing and he felt that it was beneath him to deal with the financial matters of the company. Just bringing up money issues made him lose his temper. Therefore, hearing a report that the company was on the verge of bankruptcy caused him much anger and **confusion**. The report included the **prediction** that the bankruptcy would happen before the end of the month. As usual, Philip began to sing at his colleagues in his high-pitched voice and did not bother to read the **annex** to the report. As it turned out later, the annex contained some useful information on how to avoid the bankruptcy and save the company.

Definitions: Try matching the words in the list with the appropriate definitions. If you are stuck, check the glossary in the back of the book or the passage at the top of the page.

1.	confusion _____	a.	1. a lack of understanding; uncertainty; 2. the state of being bewildered or unclear in one's mind about something
2.	genteel _____	b.	a forecast or estimation of future events
3.	prediction _____	c.	polite, refined, or respectable, often in an affected or ostentatious way
4.	annex _____	d.	(n.) a building joined to or associated with a main building; an addition to a document; (v.) to append or add as a subordinate part (especially of a document or a territory)
5.	falsetto _____	e.	for a male singer to sing notes higher than normal in range

Sentences: Try to use the words above in a sentence below. Remember that a word ending may be changed or its figure of speech slightly altered.

6.   It was funny watching Atisha sing a girly song in a(n) _____ voice.

7.   Oliver's _____ upbringing led him to always open doors for ladies.

8.   When the fire alarm blared in the mall, mass _____ broke out among the shoppers.

9.   The French apothecary and clairvoyant Nostradamus (1503-66) made _____ about the Great Fire of London (1666), the French Revolution (1789), and the advent of the atomic bomb.

10.   Upon completion of the _____, the war artifacts will be housed there.

Lesson 84

THE DETERMINED LOVER

Kyle decided to **douse** the cake with rich chocolate sauce in order to give the dessert that he cooked a more aphrodisiacal taste. Linda had not warmed up to his advances in their five previous dates; however, Kyle was a **tenacious** suitor. He showered her with **munificent** gifts. He would **extract** much pleasure from watching her admire the gifts. **Contrary** to everyone's opinion, Kyle believed that he could make Linda forget her ex-husband and fall in love with him.

Definitions: Try matching the words in the list with the appropriate definitions. If you are stuck, check the glossary in the back of the book or the passage at the top of the page.

1. tenacious _____ a. (n.) 1. a short passage taken from a piece of writing, music, or film; 2. a preparation containing the active ingredient of a substance in concentrated form; (v.) to remove or take out, especially by force

2. contrary _____ b. (of a gift or sum of money) greater or more generous than is necessary

3. extract _____ c. (adj.) 1. opposite in nature, direction, or meaning; 2. perversely inclined to do the opposite of what is expected or desired; (n.) the opposite

4. munificent _____ d. tending to keep a firm hold of something; not readily relinquishing a position, principle, or course of action

5. douse _____ e. to pour a liquid over, to drench

Sentences: Try to use the words above in a sentence below. Remember that a word ending may be changed or its figure of speech slightly altered.

6. My doctor successfully managed to _____ an ingrown toenail last week; I feel much less pain now!

7. David was very _____, refusing to give up on his dreams of being a rock star despite numerous attempts to steer him in a different direction.

8. Firefighters _____ the flames in the apartment after a fire broke out.

9. The _____ prince provided his subjects a free buffet brunch.

10. Though Most Americans think it is difficult to become rich, I believe that the _____ is true: hard work and pragmatism can help one thrive.

NEW WORDS

concur
kənˈkər

associate
əˈsōsēˌāt, -SHē-

prose
prōz

primitive
ˈprimətiv

divisive
diˈvīsiv

Lesson 85

THE PROVOCATIVE FRIEND

Even though Donald was good-natured, he enjoyed speaking about **divisive** topics that provoked anger among his friends. Last week, for example, he decided to discuss the topic of lung cancer with his friend Gerry, a chain smoker. While Gerry could politely **concur** that smoking was problematic, he could hardly stand being lectured about its health risks. In fact, such talk made Gerry not want to **associate** any further with Donald. In fact, tears welled up in Gerry's eyes as Donald spoke. Though his **primitive** instincts made him want to punch Donald, Gerry instead went home and wrote a beautiful piece of **prose** to Donald expressing his feelings about their relationship.

Definitions: Try matching the words in the list with the appropriate definitions. If you are stuck, check the glossary in the back of the book or the passage at the top of the page.

1. concur _____
2. associate _____
3. prose _____
4. primitive _____
5. divisive _____

a. 1. concerning the character of an early stage in the evolutionary or historical development of something; 2. not developed or derived from anything else

b. 1. to be of the same opinion, to agree; 2. to happen at the same time

c. written or spoken language in its typical form, without metrical structure

d. tending to cause disagreement or hostility between people

e. (adj.) joined or connected with an organization or business; (n.) a partner or colleague in business or at work; 2. a person with limited or subordinate membership in an organization; (v.) to connect someone or something with something else in one's mind

Sentences: Try to use the words above in a sentence below. Remember that a word ending may be changed or its figure of speech slightly altered.

6. Ruth's beautiful _____ was engrossing and earned her many accolades.
7. Often people of different social classes do not _____ with each other.
8. One might argue that _____ calculators have existed ever since the abacus appeared in Mesopotamia about five thousand years ago.
9. Many people would _____ that poaching safari animals is a crime.
10. Abortion is a(n) _____ issue in the United States today; people are deeply split among whether it is a woman's choice to end the life of her unborn child.

123

Lesson 86

THE OLD CIRCUS DIRECTOR

Driven by **avarice**, the circus director habitually underpaid his employees. He let them live in **miserable** conditions. Sometimes they asked for their payment, but the director would **procrastinate** and let them go hungry for days. Naturally, everyone hated him. They had no idea that he once was a **jovial** young man, full of hopes and dreams. Little by little, however, the harsh reality of being a traveling entertainer succeeded at hardening him. Aside from becoming **corrupt** and taking bribes from circus sponsors, the director's only hope for living a luxurious lifestyle and saving a hefty retirement was to prey upon his underlings at work.

NEW WORDS

miserable
ˈmiz(ə)rəbəl

avarice
ˈavəris

jovial
ˈjōvēəl

corrupt
kəˈrəpt

procrastinate
prəˈkrastəˌnāt, prō-

Definitions: Try matching the words in the list with the appropriate definitions. If you are stuck, check the glossary in the back of the book or the passage at the top of the page.

1. miserable _____
   a. (adj.) having or showing a willingness to act dishonestly in return for money or personal gain; (v.) to cause to act dishonestly in return for money or personal gain
2. avarice _____
   b. cheerful and friendly
3. jovial _____
   c. to delay or postpone action; to put off doing something
4. corrupt _____
   d. extreme greed for material gain or wealth
5. procrastinate _____
   e. 1. concerning one who is or a situation that is extremely unhappy or uncomfortable; 2. pitiably small or inadequate

Sentences: Try to use the words above in a sentence below. Remember that a word ending may be changed or its figure of speech slightly altered.

6. A _____ police officer will decide to put his or her own interests before the law.
7. Tracy's _____ led to her demise: she abandoned her friends, family, and hobbies all in pursuit of money.
8. Elmira _____ and did not begin her weekend homework assignments until late Sunday evening.
9. Sherman was a(n) _____ guy: he always enjoyed talking and joking with people at his construction company.
10. Our neighbor is _____: she quarrels with everybody and always complains about life.

NEW WORDS

merit
ˈmerit

merge
mərj

palatable
ˈpalətəbəl

precarious
priˈke(ə)rēəs

animate
ˈanəˌmit (adj.); -māt (v.)

The future of the company seemed too **precarious** on its own; therefore, the CEO decided that it needed to **merge** with a similar company to become a larger establishment. Eventually the CEO found a good fit: the other company's **merit** seemed undoubted. However, the idea of losing a part of his own power was not so **palatable** to the CEO. Nevertheless, the merge seemed to **animate** the business and things were going well. The CEO thought that now was the time to consolidate his powerful position in the new company.

Definitions: Try matching the words in the list with the appropriate definitions. If you are stuck, check the glossary in the back of the book or the passage at the top of the page.

1.	merit	_____	a.	not securely held in position; dependent on chance, uncertain
2.	merge	_____	b.	1. food or drink that is pleasant to taste; 2. an action or proposal that is acceptable or satisfactory
3.	palatable	_____	c.	to combine or cause to combine into a single entity
4.	precarious	_____	d.	(adj.) alive or having life; (v.) 1. to bring to life; to give encouragement, vigor, or renewed vigor to; 2. to give a movie or a character the appearance of movement using artistic techniques
5.	animate	_____	e.	(n.) the quality of being good or worthy; (v.) to deserve or be worthy of (typically a reward, punishment, or attention)

Sentences: Try to use the words above in a sentence below. Remember that a word ending may be changed or its figure of speech slightly altered.

6. Jacqueline earned a promotion based on her own _____: because of her industry and pragmatism, she earned a directorship position.

7. Rather than considering the ideas of Geoffrey and Andrea separately, I'd like to _____ their insights in order to create something truly innovative.

8. When the municipal government reduced funding for the subway system, the latter's survival was put in a(n) _____ state.

9. The hotel food is _____: I especially love the chocolate croissants!

10. Only when I saw the still cockroach begin to move was I convinced that it was a(n) _____ creature.

Lesson 88

MORE THAN SKIN DEEP

When Arlene fell in love with Hakim, she knew that her conservative family would **castigate** her. In fact, they probably would **expunge** her name from the family will. The fact that an Orthodox Jewish heir to a large trust fund would consider marriage to a **swarthy** Muslim, irrespective of his highly reputable profession and philanthropic endeavors, was problematic. Even pondering such an option did much to **contradict** their entrenched belief systems, and refused to **abjure** under any circumstance. All this would not stop Arlene from marrying her true love.

Definitions: Try matching the words in the list with the appropriate definitions. If you are stuck, check the glossary in the back of the book or the passage at the top of the page.

1.	castigate	_____	a.	to erase or remove completely
2.	expunge	_____	b.	to reprimand someone severely
3.	swarthy	_____	c.	to solemnly renounce a belief, cause, or claim
4.	abjure	_____	d.	dark-skinned
5.	contradict	_____	e.	to deny the truth of something by asserting the opposite; to assert the opposite of a statement made by someone

Sentences: Try to use the words above in a sentence below. Remember that a word ending may be changed or its figure of speech slightly altered.

6.   Tuan _____ his life in fashion and became an ascetic Buddhist monk.

7.   Javier's parents _____ him for staying out past his curfew and bringing a woman home with him.

8.   Vanessa's claim that she doesn't need a vacation seems to _____ the fact that she just bought a three-week travel package to tour the Alps.

9.   Even though Tonya missed two credit cards payments, she wrote to her credit union in an attempt to see if her late payments could be _____ from her record.

10.   Often villains in cartoons are depicted as enigmatic, _____ characters lurking in the shadows.

NEW WORDS

speculate
ˈspekyəˌlāt

cycle
ˈsīkəl

apex
ˈāpeks

tamper
ˈtampər

pittance
ˈpitns

Lesson 89

REALITIES OF GRADUATE SCHOOL

At the **apex** of his graduate career, John received an abundant academic stipend from the university. However, after paying for research travel fees and archival access, the money was reduced to a mere **pittance**. Unfortunately, John soon fell into a vicious **cycle** of working low-paid jobs and procrastinating the completion of his degree so that he could survive financially. He tried to **speculate** about how many more years he would need in order to finish his dissertation under these conditions. He did not want to **tamper** with progressing toward his degree; thus he had no choice but to work invidious jobs in order to pay the bills.

Definitions: Try matching the words in the list with the appropriate definitions. If you are stuck, check the glossary in the back of the book or the passage at the top of the page.

1.   speculate   _____   a.   a very small or inadequate amount of money paid to someone as an allowance or wage

2.   cycle   _____   b.   the top or highest point of something

3.   apex   _____   c.   to interfere with something in order to cause damage or make unauthorized alterations

4.   tamper   _____   d.   to form a theory about something without having firm evidence

5.   pittance   _____   e.   (n.) 1. a series of events that are regularly repeated in the same order; 2. a bicycle or tricycle; (v.) 1. to move in or follow a regularly repeated sequence of events; 2. to ride a bicycle or tricycle

Sentences: Try to use the words above in a sentence below. Remember that a word ending may be changed or its figure of speech slightly altered.

6.   When Gareth finally reached the _____ of the mountain, he took several panoramic pictures of the view.

7.   It is easy to _____ that housing prices in Singapore will rise if the population of the island-nation keeps increasing at the current rate.

8.   Tiffany was paid a(n) _____ for her many hours of hard work at the factory.

9.   Every year the Earth experiences a(n) _____ of seasons.

10.   Police detectives are not supposed to _____ with evidence in a criminal investigation.

127

Lesson 90

THE SECRET LIFE OF A DANCER

With his natural talent as a dancer, Yannis was **poised** for professional success. Everyone saw in him the next dance superstar. Nobody suspected that Yannis led a **dual** life. After each dancing performance, he would **seclude** himself in his room and take out a notebook and a pen. Writing was not only a **hobby** for him but also way to become centered. The silent process of putting his thoughts on a page would **exhilarate** him in a quiet way. He sometimes felt more alive in his room than when he was dancing on the big stage.

NEW WORDS

poised
poizd

dual
ˈd(y)o͞oəl

hobby
ˈhäbē

seclude
siˈklo͞od

exhilarate
igˈziləˌrāt

Definitions: Try matching the words in the list with the appropriate definitions. If you are stuck, check the glossary in the back of the book or the passage at the top of the page.

I.	poised	_____	a.	having a composed and self-assured manner
2.	dual	_____	b.	an activity one regularly does in one's leisure time for pleasure
3.	hobby	_____	c.	to keep (someone) away from other people
4.	seclude	_____	d.	to make (someone) feel very happy, animated, or elated
5.	exhilarate	_____	e.	consisting of two parts, elements, or aspects

Sentences: Try to use the words above in a sentence below. Remember that a word ending may be changed or its figure of speech slightly altered.

6.   Niveh has _____ roles in the university: she is both a professor who teaches and a dean who makes important administrative decisions.

7.   When I was a child, my favorite _____ was collecting baseball cards.

8.   Lisa felt _____ upon hearing that her father would be taking her to New York City on his upcoming business trip.

9.   Given all of his corporate successes, Herman is _____ to become the next CEO of the company.

10.   After losing the election, Orrin decided to _____ himself in his forest home to regroup and reassess.

Word Search

Lessons 81-90

```
P N E X T R A C T W N H O B B Y
R T O D E J L R T O A B J U R E
O N Q I X X U B I I G V P T L T
C E T R T C P S S E R I J S B J
R C J E N C U U V T T E U V Y D
A I J O V F I I N T I O M M K K
S F C D N I S D A G I F I Y M M
T I M O Y I T N E R E S L S Y D
I N C D V I C A A R E W E E Z L
N U B I M E N C T R P C D E L W
A M D P Z O E P A N L P L M D T
T V E P L R K B R U E C N N B X
E D D E P R L M D M Y T L R R Q
E M F K R E Y E N C Z L J T B M
```

1 (n.) a person who has been convicted of a felony
2 (v.) to suffocate; to stop one from acting on an emotion; to restrain or prevent
3 (v.) to delay or prevent someone or something by preventing him, her, or it
4 (adj.) not certain or fixed; provisional
5 (n.) 1. a lack of understanding; uncertainty; 2. the state of being bewildered or unclear in one's mind about something
6 (n.) a forecast or estimation of future events
7 (n.) 1. a short passage taken from a piece of writing, music, or film; 2. a preparation containing the active ingredient of a substance in concentrated form; (v.) to remove or take out, especially by force
8 (adj.) (of a gift or sum of money) greater or more generous than is necessary
9 (v.) 1. to be of the same opinion, to agree; 2. to happen at the same time
10 (adj.) tending to cause disagreement or hostility between people
11 (adj.) 1. concerning one who is or a situation that is extremely unhappy or uncomfortable; 2. pitiably small or inadequate
12 (v.) to delay or postpone action; to put off doing something
13 (n.) the quality of being good or worthy; (v.) to deserve or be worthy of (typically a reward, punishment, or attention)
14 (adj.) not securely held in position; dependent on chance, uncertain
15 (v.) to erase or remove completely
16 (v.) to solemnly renounce a belief, cause, or claim
17 (n.) 1. a series of events that are regularly repeated in the same order; 2. a bicycle or tricycle; (v.) 1. to move in or follow a regularly repeated sequence of events; 2. to ride a bicycle or tricycle
18 (n.) a very small or inadequate amount of money paid to someone as an allowance or wage
19 (n.) an activity one regularly does in one's leisure time for pleasure
20 (v.) to keep someone away from other people

Vocabulary Review
Lessons 81-90

Directions: Match each word with its best approximate definition. Note that definitions are not necessarily repeated verbatim from the lesson exercises.

1.	provocative	_____	a.	polite, refined, or respectable, often in an ostentatious way
2.	benefactor	_____	b.	a deep or seemingly bottomless pit
3.	refrain	_____	c.	written or spoken language in ordinary form
4.	abyss	_____	d.	having dark skin
5.	genteel	_____	e.	opposite in meaning or nature
6.	falsetto	_____	f.	friendly and cheerful
7.	tenacious	_____	g.	a male voice singing notes higher than normal range
8.	contrary	_____	h.	deliberately trying to evoke anger, annoyance, or some other strong reaction
9.	prose	_____	i.	a person who gives money (or something else) to help another person or cause
10.	primitive	_____	j.	to combine into a single entity
11.	avarice	_____	k.	to form a theory about something without having solid evidence
12.	jovial	_____	l.	the top or highest part of something
13.	merge	_____	m.	to reprimand severely
14.	palatable	_____	n.	concerning the early stage in the evolutionary development of something
15.	castigate	_____	o.	consisting of two parts, elements, or actions
16.	swarthy	_____	p.	extreme greed
17.	speculate	_____	q.	being composed and self-assured
18.	apex	_____	r.	keeping a firm hold of something; not easy to relinquish a position, principle, or course of action
19.	poised	_____	s.	food or drink that tastes pleasant; an action or proposal that seems satisfactory
20.	dual	_____	t.	to stop oneself from doing something

Word Roots: Unit 9

ROOTS AND THEIR MEANINGS

cur/cour:	to run	tens/ten:	to stretch
ob:	against, toward in front of	vor:	to eat
techn:	tools, skill	magna/magni:	big, great

Here are a few examples of some words that use the above roots:

courier: a messenger who transports goods or documents (eg. carries documents between places)

obviate: to avoid; prevent; remove a specific difficulty

technology: the application of scientific knowledge and/or machinery for practical purposes

tenuous: very weak or slight

voracious: wanting or devouring great quantities of something, often food

magnanimous: very generous or forgiving

Now try to fill in the table below by finding the appropriate root(s) and interpreting the meaning of each word:

Word	Root(s)	Guessed Meaning	Actual Meaning
carnivore			
technocracy			
tensile			
attenuate			
obscure			
magnificent			
current			
omnivore			
obstinate			

Specific Vocabularies 2
Transportation Words

Some Boat Terms:

- The left side of a ship when facing forward is called the **port** side
- The right side of a ship when facing forward is called the **starboard** side
- The main body of a ship, including the bottom and sides (but not including the masts or engines) is called the **hull**
- The kitchen in a boat or ship is called the **galley**
- The paddles that one uses in a boat are called **oars**
- The person in charge of a large boat or ship is called a **captain**
- A tall upright post, spar, or other structure on a boat or ship is called a **mast**

Some Airplane and Airport Terms:

- The person in charge of the airplane is called the **pilot**
- The part of the plane where the pilot sits to navigate the plane is called the **cockpit**
- The part of an airport where one picks up luggage is called a **baggage claim**
- The place at an airport where officials check passports, luggage, and goods is called **customs and immigration**
- A **layover** is a period of rest before a further stage of a journey, in the case of flying, it is a middle or intermediary location (airport) where one rests in between flights

Some Train Terms:

- The person in charge of the train is called a **conductor**
- Each car on a train is called a **coach**
- The final car on a train can be called a **caboose**
- Sometimes a train station is called a **depot**

Some Driving Terms:

- A driver whose job is to drive a limousine or town car is called a **chauffeur**
- A truck driver is called a **teamster**
- The driver's compartment of a truck, bus, or train can be called a **cab**
- The device on a vehicle that measures speed on a vehicle is called a **speedometer**
- The device on a vehicle that measures the total distance traveled is called an **odometer**

ANSWER KEY

Lesson 1

1. b
2. a
3. c
4. d
5. e
6. occupy
7. impress
8. elusive
9. derelicts
10. mettle

Lesson 2

1. a
2. e
3. d
4. c
5. b
6. melancholy
7. compel
8. urged
9. pithy
10. generosity

Lesson 3

1. a
2. c
3. e
4. b
5. d
6. languid
7. flinch
8. paragon
9. commodious
10. obdurate

Lesson 4

1. e
2. d
3. a
4. c
5. b
6. elaborate
7. assume
8. enigma
9. whet
10. mortgage

Lesson 5

1. d
2. b
3. c
4. a
5. e
6. lavish
7. invincible
8. obvious
9. typical
10. immaculate

Lesson 6

1. c
2. a
3. b
4. e
5. d
6. clamor
7. telepathic
8. trite
9. delighted
10. reeling

Lesson 7

1. c
2. e
3. a
4. b
5. d
6. token
7. lewd
8. savor
9. repose
10. premonition

Lesson 8

1. d
2. a
3. c
4. e
5. b
6. pledged
7. confidential
8. unprecedented
9. precocious
10. cherish

Lesson 9

1. b
2. a
3. c
4. d
5. e
6. conversations
7. intriguing
8. calamity
9. lax
10. ruminating

Lesson 10

1. e
2. d
3. c
4. b
5. a
6. renovate

7. tedious
8. commerce
9. heritage
10. expanse

Word Search: Lessons 1-10

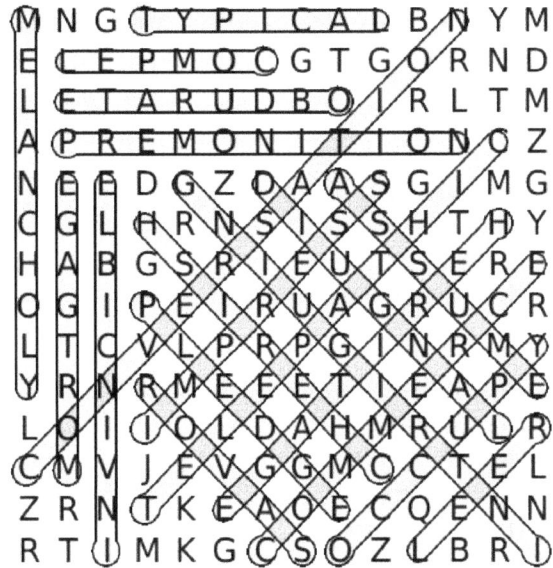

Review: Lessons 1-10

1. q
2. r
3. b
4. o
5. t
6. g
7. n
8. f
9. d
10. h
11. k
12. l
13. p
14. e
15. j
16. a
17. m
18. i
19. s
20. c

Lesson 11

1. e
2. c
3. a
4. b
5. d
6. withstand
7. zany
8. clairvoyant
9. ethical
10. din

Lesson 12

1. a
2. b
3. d
4. c
5. e
6. fasten
7. texture
8. flourish
9. sedate
10. poach

Lesson 13

1. a
2. d
3. e
4. b
5. c
6. judge
7. subsist
8. tome
9. invariably
10. procure

Lesson 14

1. b
2. e
3. a
4. d
5. c
6. antechamber

7. abundant
8. wanes
9. cooperate
10. symbol

Lesson 15

1. b
2. e
3. d
4. a
5. c
6. rotund
7. elocution
8. lamented
9. tempted
10. extrapolate

Lesson 16

1. e
2. c
3. d
4. b
5. a
6. essential
7. rescind
8. heave
9. sturdy
10. corpulent

Lesson 17

1. a
2. d
3. c
4. e
5. b
6. captivating
7. astounded
8. eventual
9. generate
10. gimmicks

Lesson 18

1. b
2. e
3. c
4. a
5. d
6. tyrannical
7. relinquish
8. entice
9. sluggard
10. submissive

Lesson 19

1. d
2. e
3. b
4. c
5. a
6. ridiculed
7. focus
8. detail
9. potent
10. tolerate

Lesson 20

1. b
2. d
3. e
4. c
5. a
6. stealthy
7. mayhem
8. notorious
9. commended
10. reminiscences

Crossword Puzzle: Lessons 11-20

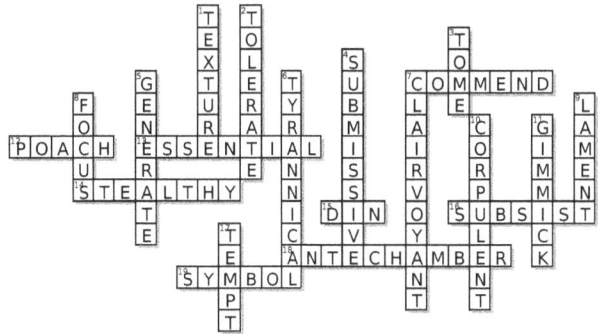

TEXTURE · TOLERATE · TYRANNIC · SUBMISSIVE · COMMEND · FOUR · GENERATE · POACH · ESSENTIAL · CLAIRVOYANT · CORPULENT · GIMMICK · LAMENT · STEALTHY · DIN · SUBSIST · TEMPT · ANTECHAMBER · SYMBOL

Review: Lessons 11-20

1. h
2. j
3. k
4. e
5. m
6. s
7. b
8. q
9. f
10. t
11. o
12. a
13. p
14. n
15. c
16. g
17. l
18. i
19. d
20. r

Lesson 21

1. a
2. b
3. c
4. e
5. d
6. repulsed
7. liberty
8. gouges

9. divulged
10. barren

Lesson 22

1. d
2. b
3. c
4. a
5. e
6. era
7. henchmen
8. stance
9. profound
10. exemplary

Lesson 23

1. c
2. b
3. e
4. d
5. a
6. veto
7. hygiene
8. specter
9. official
10. revelation

Lesson 24

1. a
2. d
3. b
4. e
5. c
6. delectable
7. melodramatic
8. decree
9. evict
10. willing

Lesson 25

1. e
2. c
3. d
4. a
5. b
6. medley
7. retaliation
8. tangible
9. contemporary
10. chronic

Lesson 26

1. e
2. d
3. b
4. c
5. a
6. rational
7. camouflage
8. vented
9. objective
10. soothsayer

Lesson 27

1. b
2. d
3. e
4. a
5. c
6. wounded
7. implied
8. opulent
9. plight
10. wreaked

Lesson 28

1. c
2. d
3. e
4. a
5. b
6. engraved

7. advocate
8. mimic
9. ordeal
10. swivel

Lesson 29

1. b
2. c
3. d
4. a
5. e
6. neophyte
7. daft
8. exonerate
9. empathy
10. divergent

Lesson 30

1. a
2. b
3. c
4. d
5. e
6. durable
7. charisma
8. judicious
9. idiosyncrasies
10. matinee

Word Search:
Lessons 21-30

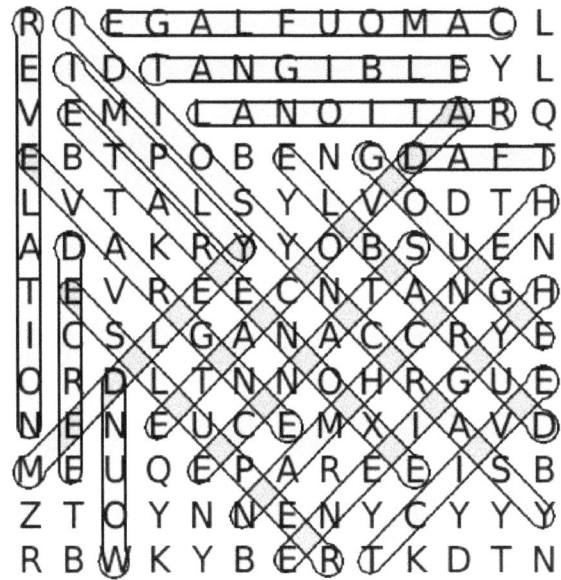

Review: Lessons 21-30

1. b
2. g
3. o
4. k
5. m
6. e
7. t
8. h
9. q
10. i
11. p
12. s
13. c
14. l
15. j
16. r
17. a
18. n
19. f
20. d

Lesson 31

1. c
2. b
3. d
4. a
5. e
6. redress
7. intersect
8. perseverance
9. qualms
10. uphold

Lesson 32

1. e
2. c
3. b
4. d
5. a
6. peculiar
7. gaping
8. negotiations
9. inadvertently
10. limber

Lesson 33

1. a
2. e
3. d
4. c
5. b
6. bliss
7. pernicious
8. gratification
9. fate
10. hesitant

Lesson 34

1. d
2. b
3. e
4. a
5. c
6. lethargic

7. stature
8. maneuver
9. accommodate
10. dexterity

Lesson 35

1. b
2. c
3. e
4. d
5. a
6. construed
7. barrier
8. expelled
9. lenient
10. goad

Lesson 36

1. a
2. d
3. b
4. c
5. e
6. vehement
7. realize
8. diverse
9. virtuous
10. apathetic

Lesson 37

1. b
2. a
3. d
4. e
5. c
6. glut
7. quell
8. reduce
9. accompanied
10. garrulous

Lesson 38

1. a
2. d
3. e
4. c
5. b
6. settle
7. foundation
8. terminate
9. void
10. inscribed

Lesson 39

1. e
2. c
3. d
4. b
5. a
6. breaches
7. lull
8. trepidation
9. rudimentary
10. obese

Lesson 40

1. d
2. a
3. c
4. b
5. e
6. presaged
7. dilapidated
8. ratify
9. manufactured
10. truce

Crossword Puzzle: Lessons 31-40

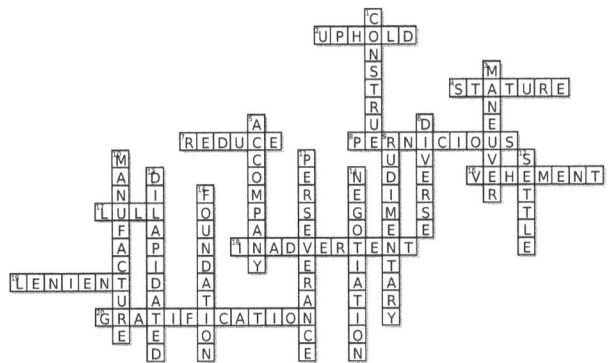

Review: Lessons 31-40

1. o
2. d
3. m
4. a
5. j
6. h
7. i
8. s
9. p
10. k
11. n
12. b
13. c
14. f
15. t
16. g
17. r
18. l
19. q
20. e

Lesson 41

1. d
2. a
3. b
4. e
5. c
6. turbulence
7. upbraided
8. uncanny

9. superficial
10. stern

Lesson 42

1. c
2. e
3. b
4. d
5. a
6. debris
7. meager
8. intricate
9. insurgent
10. hypocrisy

Lesson 43

1. c
2. d
3. e
4. b
5. a
6. pugnacious
7. souvenirs
8. barbed
9. meek
10. burnish

Lesson 44

1. e
2. a
3. c
4. b
5. d
6. quarantined
7. atrophy
8. feral
9. robust
10. pliable

Lesson 45

1. c
2. d
3. a
4. e
5. b
6. cosmic
7. random
8. anonymous
9. modicum
10. contribute

Lesson 46

1. c
2. e
3. a
4. b
5. d
6. bounty
7. deter
8. request
9. drawbacks
10. predate

Lesson 47

1. d
2. c
3. e
4. a
5. b
6. stampede
7. routine
8. mercy
9. blast
10. invade

Lesson 48

1. d
2. c
3. e
4. a
5. b

6. manifold
7. salutation
8. glint
9. communicate
10. taciturn

Lesson 49

1. b
2. d
3. a
4. e
5. c
6. incentive
7. deft
8. jeered
9. vandalized
10. blatantly

Lesson 50

1. a
2. c
3. b
4. d
5. e
6. capricious
7. mature
8. fortify
9. malign
10. murky

Word Search: Lessons 41-50

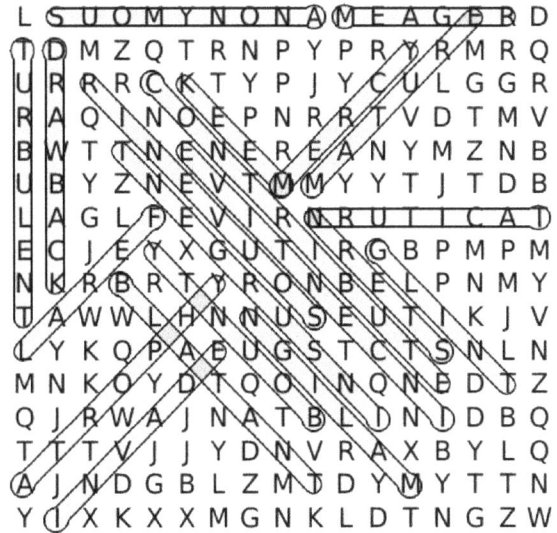

Review: Lessons 41-50

1. n
2. o
3. i
4. c
5. a
6. q
7. m
8. b
9. r
10. k
11. t
12. g
13. l
14. j
15. e
16. s
17. f
18. h
19. p
20. d

Lesson 51

1. c
2. b
3. a
4. e

5. d
6. ambled
7. crude
8. gale
9. devoted
10. plausible

Lesson 52

1. c
2. e
3. b
4. a
5. d
6. fiction
7. placid
8. thorough
9. cupidity
10. eroded

Lesson 53

1. b
2. c
3. a
4. d
5. e
6. concede
7. tact
8. terrestrial
9. nonessential
10. bided

Lesson 54

1. c
2. a
3. b
4. e
5. d
6. narrate
7. anxiety
8. consensus
9. emphasis
10. odious

Lesson 55

1. b
2. e
3. d
4. a
5. c
6. destitute
7. animosity
8. catastrophe
9. proficient
10. allay

Lesson 56

1. a
2. b
3. c
4. d
5. e
6. banished
7. banal
8. domestic
9. doze
10. jeopardy

Lesson 57

1. e
2. c
3. a
4. b
5. d
6. facilitate
7. yearn
8. boycott
9. awkward
10. fruitful

Lesson 58

1. e
2. b
3. a
4. c
5. d
6. stamina

7. penchant
8. trivial
9. debilitated
10. humidity

Lesson 59

1. e
2. b
3. a
4. c
5. d
6. familial
7. adage
8. allege
9. bulge
10. abase

Lesson 60

1. b
2. a
3. d
4. c
5. e
6. calm
7. reform
8. cowardice
9. legitimate
10. putrid

Crossword Puzzle: Lessons 51-60

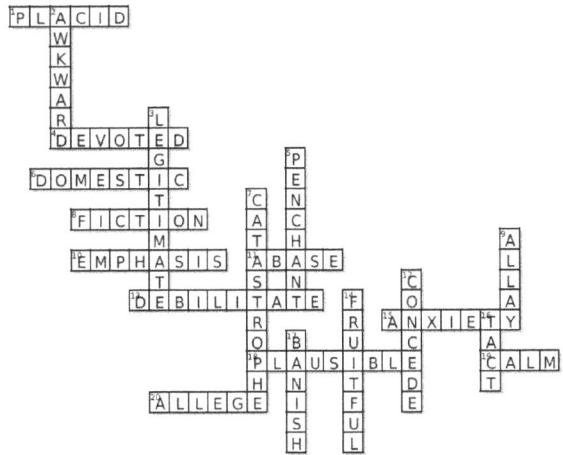

Review: Lessons 51-60

1. h
2. s
3. b
4. q
5. a
6. l
7. m
8. e
9. n
10. g
11. j
12. t
13. d
14. p
15. i
16. f
17. r
18. o
19. k
20. c

Lesson 61

1. c
2. e
3. b
4. a
5. d

6. somber
7. tardy
8. oath
9. subdue
10. cultivating

Lesson 62

1. d
2. a
3. c
4. b
5. e
6. brazen
7. presumptuously
8. furious
9. heinous
10. fostering

Lesson 63

1. a
2. e
3. b
4. c
5. d
6. pestered
7. ensnare
8. impose
9. sovereign
10. pariah

Lesson 64

1. b
2. c
3. a
4. d
5. e
6. boisterous
7. compassion
8. acrid
9. repugnant
10. omit

Lesson 65

1. d
2. b
3. c
4. e
5. a
6. zenith
7. entertain
8. indulgent
9. wither
10. instance

Lesson 66

1. e
2. a
3. d
4. c
5. b
6. hospitable
7. encompass
8. scanty
9. luminous
10. pretentious

Lesson 67

1. e
2. b
3. c
4. a
5. d
6. progressive
7. dissonance
8. sanitary
9. prudish
10. replica

Lesson 68

1. b
2. c
3. a
4. d
5. e

6. sacred
7. accede
8. evoked
9. preponderance
10. stupefied

Lesson 69

1. c
2. a
3. e
4. d
5. b
6. eminent
7. mischief
8. contempt
9. process
10. stolid

Lesson 70

1. e
2. d
3. a
4. b
5. c
6. collateral
7. tailor
8. massive
9. variety
10. inquisitive

Word Search: Lessons 61-70

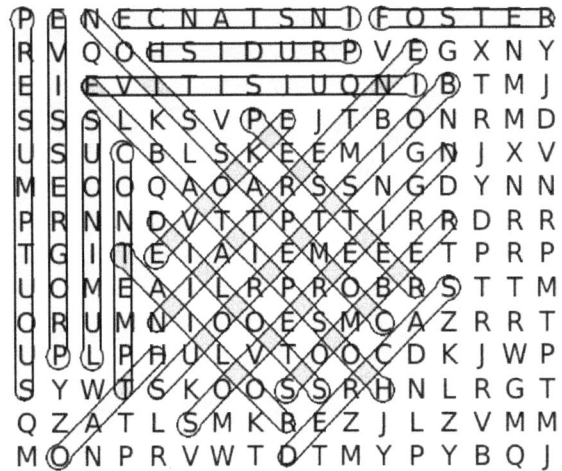

Review: Lessons 61-70

1. s
2. h
3. c
4. k
5. b
6. g
7. j
8. l
9. p
10. o
11. e
12. d
13. a
14. t
15. m
16. i
17. q
18. f
19. n
20. r

Lesson 71

1. a
2. c
3. d
4. e
5. b

6. preposterous
7. sentries
8. incredulous
9. insinuate
10. seer

Lesson 72

1. c
2. b
3. d
4. a
5. e
6. expenditures
7. chaffed
8. smite
9. onus
10. statute

Lesson 73

1. a
2. c
3. d
4. b
5. e
6. express
7. brawn
8. connotation
9. sage
10. untainted

Lesson 74

1. e
2. d
3. a
4. c
5. b
6. nutritious
7. diminish
8. brash
9. phobias
10. forestall

Lesson 75

1. e
2. d
3. b
4. a
5. c
6. equitable
7. portentous
8. charred
9. donates
10. inextricably

Lesson 76

1. c
2. b
3. e
4. d
5. a
6. negligent
7. populated
8. prestidigitation
9. enormous
10. appropriate

Lesson 77

1. e
2. d
3. b
4. a
5. c
6. requisition
7. propaganda
8. fallacy
9. somnolent
10. concocted

Lesson 78

1. d
2. e
3. c
4. b
5. a
6. dormant

7. ideal
8. exist
9. scathing
10. unswerving

Lesson 79

1. a
2. c
3. b
4. e
5. d
6. olfactory
7. transpired
8. ravenous
9. conniving
10. tradition

Lesson 80

1. a
2. e
3. b
4. c
5. d
6. shunned
7. null
8. adept
9. ransacked
10. malicious

Crossword Puzzle: Lessons 71-80

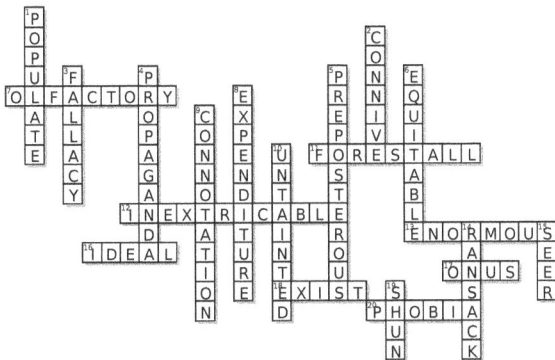

Review: Lessons 71-80

1. g
2. q
3. n
4. m
5. a
6. t
7. s
8. k
9. o
10. b
11. f
12. e
13. r
14. j
15. l
16. c
17. d
18. p
19. h
20. i

Lesson 81

1. e
2. d
3. a
4. b
5. c
6. stifling
7. provocative
8. exotic
9. benefactors
10. felon

Lesson 82

1. d
2. a
3. c
4. e
5. b
6. refrain
7. demote
8. impede
9. abyss
10. tentative

Lesson 83

1. a
2. c
3. b
4. d
5. e
6. falsetto
7. genteel
8. confusion
9. predictions
10. annex

Lesson 84

1. d
2. c
3. a
4. b
5. e
6. extract
7. tenacious
8. doused
9. munificent
10. contrary

Lesson 85

1. b
2. e
3. c
4. a
5. d
6. prose
7. associate
8. primitive
9. concur
10. divisive

Lesson 86

1. e
2. d
3. b
4. a
5. c
6. corrupt
7. avarice
8. procrastinated
9. jovial
10. miserable

Lesson 87

1. e
2. c
3. b
4. a
5. d
6. merit
7. merge
8. precarious
9. palatable
10. animate

Lesson 88

1. b
2. a
3. d
4. c
5. e
6. abjured
7. castigated
8. contradict
9. expunged
10. swarthy

Lesson 89

1. d
2. e
3. b
4. c
5. a
6. apex
7. speculate
8. pittance
9. cycle
10. tamper

149

Lesson 90

1. a
2. e
3. b
4. c
5. d
6. dual
7. hobby
8. exhilarated
9. poised
10. seclude

Word Search: Lessons 81-90

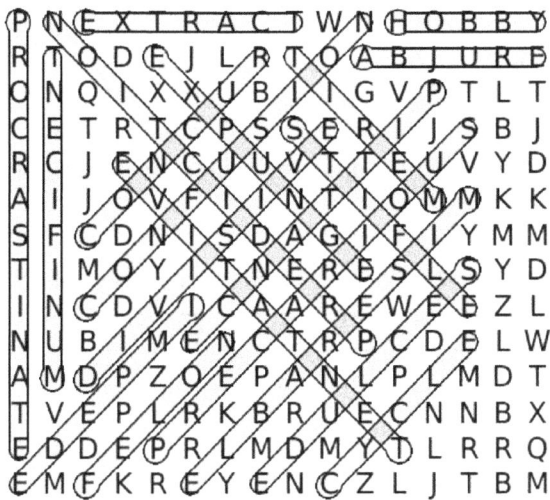

Review: Lessons 81-90

1. h
2. i
3. t
4. b
5. a
6. g
7. r
8. e
9. c
10. n
11. p
12. f
13. j
14. s
15. m
16. d
17. k
18. l
19. q
20. o

GLOSSARY

This glossary contains definitions of the new words from every lesson contained in this book. Please note that not every meaning of each word is contained in this glossary. Generally, only the most commonly used meanings of the words below are defined.

All entries in the glossary take the following form:

word (lesson): (part of speech) definition

Key for parts of speech:
adj. = adjective   n. = noun   v. = verb

A

abase (59): (v.) to behave in such a way as to degrade or belittle someone

abjure (88): (v.) to solemnly renounce a belief, cause, or claim

abundant (14): (adj.) existing or available in great quantities

abyss (82): (n.) a deep or seemingly bottomless chasm

accede (68): (v.) to assent or agree to a request, demand, or treaty

accommodate (34): (v.) 1. to provide lodging or sufficient space for; 2. to fit in with the wishes or needs of

accompany (37): (v.) to go somewhere with someone as a companion or escort; to be present or occur at the same time as something else; to provide something as a complement or addition to something else

acrid (64): (adj.) having an irritatingly strong and unpleasant taste or smell

adage (59): (n.) a proverb or short statement expressing a general truth

adept (80): (adj.) very skilled or proficient at something

advocate (28): (n.) a person who publicly supports or recommends a particular cause or policy; 2. a person who pleads on someone else's behalf; (v.) to publicly recommend or support

allay (55): (v.) (of a fear, suspicion, or worry) to diminish or put at rest

allege (59): (v.) to claim or assert that someone has done something illegal or wrong, typically without proof

amble (51): (v.) to walk or move at a slow, relaxed pace

animate (87): (adj.) alive or having life; (v.) 1. to bring to life; to give encouragement, vigor, or renewed vigor to; 2. to give a movie or a character the appearance of movement using artistic techniques

animosity (55): (n.) strong hostility

annex (83): (n.) a building joined to or associated with a main building; an addition to a document; (v.) to append or add as a subordinate part (especially of a document or a territory)

anonymous (45): (adj.) (of a person) not identified by name, or of unknown name

antechamber (14): (n.) a small room leading to a big one

anxiety (54): (n.) a feeling of worry, unease, or nervousness, typically about an imminent event or one with an uncertain outcome

apathy (36): (n.) lack of interest, enthusiasm, or concern

apex (89): (n.) the top or highest point of something

appropriate (76): (adj.) suitable or proper in the circumstances; (v.) 1. to take something for one's use, typically without permission; 2. to devote money or assets to a special purpose

associate (85): (adj.) joined or connected with an organization or business; (n.) a partner or colleague in business or at work; 2. a person with limited or subordinate membership in an organization; (v.) to connect someone or something with something else in one's mind

assume (4): (v.) 1. to suppose to be the case without proof; 2. to take or begin to have power or responsibility; 3. to seize power or control over something; 4. to take on a characteristic or quality for a role

astound (17): (v.) to shock or greatly surprise

atrophy (44): (v.) 1. for a body tissue to waste away, typically due to the degeneration of cells; 2. to gradually decline in effectiveness or vigor due to underuse or neglect

avarice (86): (n.) extreme greed for material gain or wealth

awkward (57): (adj.) 1. causing difficulty, hard to do or deal with; 2. causing or feeling embarrassment or inconvenience; 3. not smooth or grateful

B

banal (56): (adj.) lacking in originality and thus being obvious or boring

banish (56): (v.) to send someone away from a country or place as official punishment

barbed (43): (adj.) having sharp projections on an object so as to make extraction difficult; deliberately hurtful

barren (21): (adj.) empty, bleak, and lifeless; (of land) too poor to produce substantial vegetation

barrier (35): (n.) an object that prevents movement or access

benefactor (81): (n.) a person who gives money or other aid to help a person or cause

bide (53): (v.) to remain or stay somewhere

blast (47): (n.) 1. a destructive wave of compressed air spreading outward from an explosion; 2. a strong gust of wind or air; 3. a single loud noise emanating from a horn or other musical instrument; (v.) 1. to blow up or break apart something with explosives; 2. to make or cause to make a loud continuous musical or other noise

blatant (49): (adj.) typically bad behavior done openly and unashamedly

bliss (33): (n.) perfect happiness; great joy

boisterous (64): (adj.) 1. (of a person, event, or occasion) energetic, noisy, and cheerful; 2. (of wind, weather, or water) wild or stormy

bounty (46): (n.) 1. generosity, liberality; abundance; 2. a monetary gift or reward given by a government, usually for killing or capturing a criminal

boycott (57): (n.) a punitive ban that forbids relations with certain groups, cooperation with a policy, or the handling of goods; (v.) to withdraw from commercial or social relations with a country, organization, or person as a punishment or protest

brash (74): (adj.) self-assertive in a rude, overbearing, or noisy way; overbearing

brawn (73): (n.) physical strength (in contrast to intelligence)

brazen (62): (adj.) bold and without shame

breach (39): (n.) 1. an act of breaking a law, agreement, or code of conduct; 2. a gap in a wall, barrier, or defense made by an army; (v.) to break a law, agreement, or code of conduct; 2. to make a gap in and break through a wall, barrier, or defense

bulge (59): (n.) a rounded swelling or protuberance that distorts a flat surface; (v.) to swell or protrude to an unnatural or incongruous extent

burnish (43): (v.) to polish

C

calamity (9): (n.) a disaster

calm (60): (adj.) 1. (of a person) not showing signs of anger, nervousness, or other emotions, 2. pleasantly free from wind; (n.) 1. the absence of violent confrontational activity within a place or group; 2. the absence of wind; (v.) to make someone quiet; soothe

camouflage (26): (n.) the disguising of people (especially military personnel), equipment, and installations by covering them to make them blend in with natural surroundings; material used for such disguise; an animal's covering that lets it blend in with natural surroundings; (v.) to hide or disguise the presence of a person, animal, or object; to conceal the existence of something undesirable

caprice (50): (n.) a sudden and unaccountable change of mood or behavior

captivating (17): (adj.) capable of attracting and holding interest

castigate (88): (v.) to reprimand someone severely

catastrophe (55): (n.) an event causing great and often sudden damage or suffering

chaff (72): (v.) to tease

char (75): (v.) to partially burn an object as to blacken its surface

charisma (30): (n.) compelling attractiveness or charm that can inspire others

cherish (8): (v.) to protect and care for something or someone lovingly; to hold dear

chronic (25): (adj.) persisting for a long time or constantly recurring

clairvoyant (11): (adj.) having the ability to see or predict events in the future beyond normal sense; (n.) a person who claims to have the supernatural ability to see events in the future beyond normal sense

clamor (6): (n.) a loud and confused noise, perhaps protest; (v.) to shout loudly and insistently as a group, often to protest or demand

collateral (70): (n.) something pledged as security for repayment of a loan

commend (20): (v.) to praise formally or officially; to present as suitable for approval or acceptance; recommend

commerce (10): (v.) 1. the act of buying and selling, trade; 2. social dealings between people

commodious (3): (adj.) roomy and comfortable

communicate (48): (v.) to share or exchange information, news, or ideas

compassion (64): (n.) sympathetic pity and concern for the suffering and misfortunes of others

compel (2): (v.) to force or oblige someone or something; to bring about something by the use of pressure or force

concede (53): (v.) 1. to admit that something is true or valid after first denying or resisting it; 2. to surrender or yield something that one possesses or desires

concoct (77): (v.) 1. to make a dish or meal by combining various ingredients; 2. to create or devise a story or plan

concur (85): (v.) 1. to be of the same opinion, to agree; 2. to happen at the same time

confidential (8): (adj.) intended to be kept secret

confusion (83): (n.) 1. a lack of understanding; uncertainty; 2. the state of being bewildered or unclear in one's mind about something

connive (79): (v.) to secretly allow something immoral, illegal, wrong, or harmful to occur (often conspiring with others)

connotation (73): (n.) an idea or feeling that a word evokes in addition to its literal meaning

consensus (54): (n.) a general agreement

construe (35): (v.) to interpret a word or action in a particular way

contemporary (25): (adj.) 1. living or occurring at the same time; 2. belonging or occurring in the present; (n.) 1. a person or living thing existing at the same time as another; 2. a person of roughly the same age as another

contempt (69): (n.) 1. a feeling that a person is beneath consideration, deserving scorn, or unworthy; 2. a disregard for something that should be taken into account

contradict (88): (v.) to deny the truth of something by asserting the opposite; to assert the opposite of a statement made by someone

contrary (84): (adj.) 1. opposite in nature, direction, or meaning; 2. perversely inclined to do the opposite of what is expected or desired; (n.) the opposite

contribute (45): (v.) to give (something, often money) in order to help achieve or provide something

conversation (9): (n.) an informal exchange of ideas by spoken words

cooperate (14): (v.) to act jointly and work toward the same end; to assist someone (or an organization) and comply with his or her (its) requests

corpulent (16): (adj.) fat (describing a person)

corrupt (86): (adj.) having or showing a willingness to act dishonestly in return for money or personal gain; (v.) to cause to act dishonestly in return for money or personal gain

cosmic (45): (adj.) of or relating to the universe or things beyond Earth

cowardice (60): (n.) lack of bravery

crude (51): (adj.) 1. in a natural or raw state; unrefined; 2.constructed in a rudimentary way; 3. (of a person) especially offensive or rude, especially in a sexual way

cultivate (61): (v.) 1. to prepare and use land for crops or gardening; 2. to acquire and develop a quality, skill, or sentiment

cupidity (52): (n.) greed for money or possessions

cycle (89): (n.) 1. a series of events that are regularly repeated in the same order; 2. a bicycle or tricycle; (v.) 1. to move in or follow a regularly repeated sequence of events; 2. to ride a bicycle or tricycle

D

daft (29): (adj.) silly; foolish

debilitate (58): (adj.) 1. to make someone weak and infirm; 2. to hinder, delay, or weaken

debris (42): (n.) scattered fragments of something wrecked or destroyed

decree (24): (n.) an official order issued by a ruler or legal authority

deft (49): (adj.) neatly skillful and quick in one's movements

delectable (24): (adj.) delicious; tasty

delight (6): (n.) a great pleasure; (v.) to please (someone) greatly; to take great pleasure in something

demote (82): (v.) to give someone a lower rank or less senior position, usually as a punishment

derelict (1): (adj.) in poor condition due to neglect and/or disuse; (n.) 1. a person lacking a job, home, or property; 2. a person negligent in doing his or her duty

destitute (55): (adj.) lacking the basic necessities in life

detail (19): (n.) an individual feature, fact, or item; (v.) to give particulars of, describe item by item

deter (46): (v.) to discourage someone from doing something, typically by instilling doubt or fear

devoted (51): (adj.) very loving and loyal

dexterity (34): (n.) skill at performing tasks, especially with the hands

dilapidated (40): (adj.) a building or object in a state of disrepair or ruin as a result of age or neglect

diminish (74): (v.) to make or become less

din (11): (n.) a loud, unpleasant, and prolonged noise

dissonance (67): (n.) lack of harmony between two or more musical notes; a tension resulting from a combination of two or more unsuitable elements

divergent (29): (adj.) tending to be different or to develop in different directions

diverse (36): (adj.) showing a great deal of variety; very different

divisive (85): (adj.) tending to cause disagreement or hostility between people

divulge (21): (v.) to make private or sensitive information known

domestic (56): (adj.) 1. of or relating to running a home or family relations; 2. existing or occurring inside a particular country

donate (75): (v.) 1. to give one's money or goods for a cause, especially a charity; 2. to allow the removal of one's blood or organ(s) from one's body for transplant or transfusion

dormant (78): (adj.) 1. (of an animal) having normal physical functions suspended as if in a deep sleep; 2. (of a volcano) temporarily inactive; 3. (of a disease) showing no symptoms but liable to recur

douse (84): (v.) to pour a liquid over, to drench

doze (56): (v.) to sleep lightly

drawback (46): (n.) a feature that renders something less acceptable; a disadvantage or problem

dual (90): (adj.) consisting of two parts, elements, or aspects

durable (30): (adj.) able to withstand wear, pressure, or damage

E

elaborate (4): (adj.) 1. having many carefully arranged or designed details; detailed in plan or design; 2. lengthy and exaggerated; (v.) to add more detail concerning something already said

elocution (15): (n.) the skill of articulate and expressive speech

elusive (1): (adj.) hard to find, catch, or achieve

eminent (69): (adj.) characterizing a person who is famous or respected within a certain field or profession

empathy (29): (n.) the ability to understand and share the feelings of another

emphasis (54): (n.) special importance, value, or prominence given to something

encompass (66): (v.) to surround or enclose within; to include comprehensively

engrave (28): (v.) to cut or carve a text or design on the surface of a hard object

enigma (4): (adj.) a mystery

enormous (76): (adj.) very large in size, quantity, or extent

ensnare (63): (v.) to catch in or as in a trap

entertain (65): (v.) 1. to provide someone with amusement or enjoyment; 2. to give attention or consideration to an idea, suggestion, or feeling

entice (18): (v.) to attract or tempt by offering pleasure or advantage

equitable (75): (adj.) fair and impartial

era (22): (adj.) a long and distinct period of history with a particular feature or characteristic

erode (52): (v.) to gradually wear away (usually of water, wind, or other natural elements)

essential (16): (adj.) absolutely necessary; extremely important

ethical (11): (adj.) of or relating to moral principles; morally correct

eventual (17): (adj.) occurring at the end or as a result of a sequence of events; ultimate; final

evict (24): (v.) to expel someone from a property with the assistance of the law

evoke (68): (v.) to bring or call to mind; to elicit a response; to invoke a spirit or deity

exemplary (22): (adj.) 1. serving as a desirable model; representing the best of its kind; 2. (in terms of punishment) serving as a warning or deterrent

exhilarate (90): (v.) to make (someone) feel very happy, animated, or elated

exist (78): (v.) 1. to have objective reality or being; 2. to live (under especially adverse conditions)

exonerate (29): (v.) to absolve someone from blame for a wrongdoing

exotic (81): (adj.) originating in or characteristic of a foreign country; appealing because of having come from a far away place

expanse (10): (n.) an area of something that contains a wide and continuous surface; the distance to which something can stretch

expel (35): (v.) to deprive someone membership or involvement in a school or organization; to force someone to leave a place

expenditure (72): (n.) the action of spending funds

express (73): (adj.) operating at high speed; (n.) a rapid moving vehicle or delivery service; (v.) 1. to convey a thought or feeling in words or by gestures and conduct; 2. to send quickly or at high speed

expunge (88): (v.) to erase or remove completely

extract (84): (n.) 1. a short passage taken from a piece of writing, music, or film; 2. a preparation containing the active ingredient of a substance in concentrated form; (v.) to remove or take out, especially by force

extrapolate (15): (v.) to extend the application of a method or a conclusion to an unknown trend by assuming that existing trends will continue or that similar methods will be applicable

F

facilitate (57): (v.) to make an action or process easier

fallacy (77): (n.) a mistaken belief, especially one founded on unsound argument

falsetto (83): (adj.) for a male singer to sing notes higher than normal in range

familial (59): (adj.) of, relating to, or concerning a family and its members

fasten (12): (v.) to close or join securely; to fix in place; to fix one's attention on something

fate (33): (n.) the development of events beyond a person's control, regarded as determined by a supernatural power

felon (81): (n.) a person who has been convicted of a felony

feral (44): (adj.) (usually of an animal) in a wild state, especially after escaping domesticity or captivity

fiction (52): (n.) prose literature in the form of novels that describes imaginary people and events

flinch (3): (n.) a fast, nervous movement of the body as an instinctive response to pain, surprise, or fear; (v.) to make a fast, nervous movement of the body as an instinctive response to pain, surprise, or fear

flourish (12): (n.) an elaborate literary or rhetorical expression; (v.) for a person or other living organism to grow in a healthy or vigorous way, usually as the result of a favorable environment

focus (19): (n.) 1. the center of interest or activity; 2. the state or quality of having or producing clear visual definition; (v). 1. to adapt to the prevailing level of light so as to see clearly; 2. to pay attention to (focus on)

forestall (74): (v.) to prevent an event or action from happening by taking advance action; an act to delay

fortify (50): (v.) to strengthen a place with defensive works so as to protect it from attack; to strengthen or invigorate someone mentally or physically

foster (62): (v.) to encourage or promote the development of something; to develop a feeling or idea within oneself

foundation (38): (n.) 1. the lowest load-bearing part of a building, typically underground; 2. the underlying basis or principle for something; 3. an institution or organization with an endowment

fruitful (57): (adj.) producing much fruit, fertile; producing good or helpful results

furious (62): (adj.) extremely angry

G

gale (51): (n.) a very strong wind

gape (32): (v.) to stare with one's mouth open wide, typically in amazement or wonder; to become wide or open

garrulous (37): (adj.) excessively talkative in a roundabout way, especially on trivial matters

generate (17): (v.) to produce; to cause a particular situation or emotion to come about

generosity (2): (n.) the quality of being kind, giving, and helpful

genteel (83): (adj.) polite, refined, or respectable, often in an affected or ostentatious way

gimmick (17): (n.) a device or trick aimed at attracting attention, publicity, or business

glint (48): (n.) a small flash of light; (of one's eyes) a shine with a particular emotion; (v.) to give out or reflect small flashes of light

glut (37): (n.) an excessively abundant supply of something

goad (35): (v.) to provoke or annoy someone so as to stimulate some action or reaction

gouge (21): (v.) to scoop; to make a groove, hole, or indentation; to cut or force something out roughly or brutally

gratification (33): (n.) pleasure, typically when attained from the satisfaction of a desire

H

heave (16): (n.) a push, haul, or throw requiring great effort; (v.) 1. to push, haul, or throw with great effort; 2. to produce a sigh

heinous (62): (adj.) a person, wrongful act, or crime that is utterly odious or wicked

henchman (22): (n.) a faithful supporter, especially one inclined to engage in unethical behavior by way of practice

heritage (10): (n.) valued objects and qualities like cultural traditions, unsullied countryside, and historic buildings that have been passed down over generations

hesitant (33): (adj.) tentative, unsure, or slow in acting or speaking

hobby (90): (n.) an activity one regularly does in one's leisure time for pleasure

hospitable (66): (adj.) friendly and welcoming to guests; (of an environment) pleasant and favorable for living in

humidity (58): (n.) concerning the amount of water vapor in the air

hygiene (23): (n.) conditions or practices conducive to maintaining health and preventing disease, especially through cleanliness

hypocrisy (42): (n.) the practice of claiming to have certain moral standards or beliefs to which one's behavior does not conform

I

ideal (78): (adj.) satisfying one's conception of what is perfect or most suitable; (n.) a person or thing regarded as perfect; a standard of perfection or principle to be aimed at

idiosyncrasy (30): (n.) a mode of behavior or way of thought peculiar to an individual; a distinctive characteristic peculiar to a person or thing

immaculate (5): (adj.) 1. perfectly neat or clean; 2. free of mistakes

impede (82): (v.) to delay or prevent someone or something by preventing him, her, or it

imply (27): (v.) to strongly suggest the truth, existence, or logical consequence of something

impose (63): (v.) 1. to force something unwelcome or unfamiliar to be accepted or put into place; 2. to take advantage of someone by demanding their attention or commitment

impress (1): (v.) 1. to make one feel admiration and respect; 2. to make a mark upon an object by using a stamp or seal; 3. to fix an idea in someone's mind

inadvertent (32): (adj.) not resulting from or achieved through deliberate planning

incentive (49): (n.) a thing that motivates or encourages one to do something

incredulous (71): (adj.) a person who is unable or unwilling to believe something

indulgent (65): (adj.) having or indicating a tendency to be overly generous or lenient with someone

inextricable (75): (adj.) impossible to disentangle or separate; impossible to escape from

inquisitive (70): (adj.) curious and asking many questions

inscribe (38): (v.) to write or carve words or symbols on something, especially as a permanent record

insinuate (71): (v.) to suggest or hint at (something bad or reprehensible) in an unpleasant way

instance (65): (n.) an example or single occurrence of something

insurgent (42): (adj.) rising in active revolt; (n.) a rebel or revolutionary

intersect (31): (v.) to divide something by passing or lying across it

intricate (42): (adj.) very complicated or detailed

intriguing (9): (adj.) arousing curiosity or interest; fascinating

invade (47): (v.) for an armed forces to enter a region and occupy it; to enter an area in large numbers; for a disease to spread into an organism or body part; to encroach or intrude on

invariable (13): (adj.) unchanging

invincible (5): (adj.) too powerful to be overcome or defeated

J

jeer (49): (n.) a rude, mocking remark; (v.) to make rude and mocking comments, typically in a rude manner

jeopardy (56): (n.) danger of loss, harm, or failure

jovial (86): (adj.) cheerful and friendly

judge (13): (n.) an individual with the authority to decide cases in courts of law; an individual who decides the results of competition or infractions of rules; (v.) 1. to form an opinion or conclusion about; 2. to decide a case in court; 3. to decide the results of a competition

judicious (30): (adj.) having done or showing good judgment or sense

L

lament (15): (n.) 1. a passionate expression of grief or sorrow; 2. a song or poem expressing sorrow; 3. an expression of disappointment; (v.) to mourn a person's death

languid (3): (adj.) 1. concerning a person, manner, or gesture showing a lack of exertion or effort; lacking energy; 2. a time period that's peaceful or pleasantly lazy

lavish (5): (adj.) extremely rich, luxurious, or elaborate; characterizing a person who is very generous or extravagant; given to profusion; (v.) to heap generous quantities upon

lax (9): (adj.) not strict, severe, or careful; loose; relaxed

legitimate (60): (adj.) conforming to the law or rules; (v.) to justify or make lawful

lenient (35): (adj.) (of punishment or a person in authority) tending to be permissive, merciful or tolerant

lethargic (34): (adj.) sluggish, apathetic

lewd (7): (adj.) offensive and crude in a sexual way

liberty (21): (n.) 1. the state of being free within society; the state of not being incarcerated or enslaved; 2. the power to act as one pleases

limber (32): (adj.) lithe; supple

lull (39): (n.) a temporary interval of quiet or lack of activity; (v.) to calm or send to sleep typically with soothing sounds or movements

luminous (66): (adj.) full of light; shedding light; bright or shining, especially in the dark

M

malicious (80): (adj.) characterized by an intention to do harm

malign (50): (adj.) evil in nature or effect, malevolent; (v.) to speak about another in a spitefully cruel manner

maneuver (34): (n.) a movement or series of moves that requires skill and care; 2. a carefully planned scheme or action; (v.) 1. to move skillfully or carefully; 2. to carefully guide or manipulate something or someone to achieve an end

manifold (48): (adj.) many and various

manufacture (40): (n.) the making of articles on a large scale using machinery; (v.) 1. to make something on a large scale using machinery; 2. to invent or fabricate evidence or a story

massive (70): (adj.) exceptionally large, heavy, solid, or important

matinee (30): (n.) a daytime theater performance or movie showing

mature (50): (adj.) fully developed physically; full-grown; (v.) to become physically or emotionally developed

mayhem (20): (adj.) damaging or violent disorder; chaos

meager (42): (adj.) lacking in quantity or quality

medley (25): (n.)a varied mixture of people or things; a mixture

meek (43): (adj.) quiet, gentle, submissive; easily imposed upon

melancholy (2): (adj.) having or feeling sad and pensive; (n.) a feeling of sadness, typically with no apparent cause

melodramatic (24): (adj.) overly emotional or dramatic

mercy (47): (n.) compassion or forgiveness shown toward someone whom it is within one's power to punish or harm

merge (87): (v.) to combine or cause to combine into a single entity

merit (87): (n.) the quality of being good or worthy; (v.) to deserve or be worthy of (typically a reward, punishment, or attention)

mettle (1): (n.) one's ability to manage a difficult situation in an enthusiastic and spirited way

mimic (28): (v.) to imitate someone's actions or words, typically with an attempt to ridicule

mischief (69): (n.) playful behavior often involved in troublemaking and usually exhibited by children; playfulness intended to tease, mock, and create trouble; harm or trouble caused by something

miserable (86): (adj.) 1. concerning one who is or a situation that is extremely unhappy or uncomfortable; 2. pitiably small or inadequate

modicum (45): (n.) a small quantity of a particular thing, especially one that is valuable

mortgage (4): (n.) the charging of property (usually a home) by a debtor to a creditor as security for a debt; (v.) to convey property to a creditor as security on a loan

munificent (84): (adj.) (of a gift or sum of money) greater or more generous than is necessary

murky (50): (adj.) dark and gloomy, usually because of thick mist

N

narrate (54): (v.) to give a spoken or written account of something

negligent (76): (adj.) failing to take proper care in doing something

negotiation (32): (n.) discussion aimed at reaching an agreement

neophyte (29): (adj.) a person who is new to a subject, skill, or belief

nonessential (53): (adj.) not absolutely necessary

notorious (20): (adj.) famous or well-known, especially for a bad deed or quality

null (80): (adj.) 1. having no legal or binding force; invalid; 2. having or associated with the value zero

nutritious (74): (adj.) nourishing and efficient as food

O

oath (61): (n.) a solemn promise, often invoking a divine witness, regarding one's future behavior or action

obdurate (3): (adj.) stubbornly refusing to change one's opinion or course of action

obese (39): (adj.) grossly fat or overweight

objective (26): (adj.) not influenced by personal feelings; (n.) a thing aimed at or sought; a goal

obvious (5): (adj.) easily perceived or understood; easily apparent; self-evident; blatant

occupy (1): (v.) 1. to reside or have one's business in; to be situated in; to fill or take up; to hold (a job); 2. (military) to enter, take control of, and remain in a place

odious (54): (adj.) extremely unpleasant; repulsive

official (23): (adj.) relating to an authority or body and its duties, actions, or responsibilities; (n.) a person holding public office and having official duties

olfactory (79): (adj.) of or relating to the sense of smell

omit (64): (v.) to leave out or exclude, either intentionally or deliberately

onus (72): (n.) used to refer to something that is one's duty or responsibility

opulent (27): (adj.) ostentatiously rich and luxurious; extremely lavish

ordeal (28): (n.) a painful or horrific experience, often one that is protracted

P

palatable (87): (adj.) 1. food or drink that is pleasant to taste; 2. an action or proposal that is acceptable or satisfactory

paragon (3): (n.) a person or thing regarded as the perfect example of something

pariah (63): (n.) an outcast

peculiar (32): (adj.) 1. strange or odd; unusual; 2. belonging exclusively to

penchant (58): (n.) a strong and habitual liking for something or tendency to do something

pernicious (33): (adj.) having a harmful effect, especially in a harmful or subtle way

perseverance (31): (n.) steadfastness in doing something despite difficulty or delay in achieving success

pester (63): (v.) to trouble or annoy someone with frequent interruptions or requests

phobia (74): (n.) an extreme or irrational fear of or aversion to something

pithy (2): (adj.) brief and forceful in expression

pittance (89): (n.) a very small or inadequate amount of money paid to someone as an allowance or wage

placid (52): (adj.) a person or animal not easily upset or excited; (of a place or stretch of water) calm and peaceful, with little movement or activity

plausible (51): (adj.) an argument or statement that seems reasonable or logical

pledge (8): (n.) 1. a solemn promise or understanding; 2. a promise of a donation to a charity; (v.) 1. to commit by solemn promise; 2. to formally declare or promise that something will be the case

pliable (44): (adj.) 1. easily bent; flexible; 2. easily influenced

plight (27): (n.) a difficult, dangerous, or unfortunate situation

poach (12): (v.) 1. to illegally hunt or catch; 2. to acquire in a secretive way

poised (90): (adj.) having a composed and self-assured manner

populate (76): (v.) to fill with people; to form the population of a particular town, area, or country

163

portentous (75): (adj.) ominously significant or important; momentous

potent (19): (adj.) having great power, influence, or effect

precarious (87): (adj.) not securely held in position; dependent on chance, uncertain

precocious (8): (adj.) (of a child) having developed certain skills or abilities at an earlier age than usual; indicative of early development

predate (46): (v.) to exist or occur at a date earlier than something

prediction (83): (n.) a forecast or estimation of future events

premonition (7): (n.) a strong feeling that something (typically unpleasant) is about to happen

preponderance (68): (n.) the fact or quality of being great in number, quantity, extent, or importance

preposterous (71): (adj.) absurd or ridiculous; contrary to common sense

presage (40): (n.) a sign or warning that something (typically bad) will happen; an omen or portent; (v.) (of an event) to be a sign that something (typically bad) will happen

prestidigitation (76): (n.) slight of hand; legerdemain

presumptuous (62): (adj.) (concerning a person and his or her behavior) failing to observe the limits of what is deemed appropriate

pretentious (66): (adj.) attempting to impress by assuming greater importance, talent, culture, or credibility than one actually possesses

primitive (85): (adj.) 1. concerning the character of an early stage in the evolutionary or historical development of something; 2. not developed or derived from anything else

process (69): (n.) a series of actions or steps taken in order to achieve a particular end; (v.) to perform a series of mechanical or chemical operations on something in order to change or preserve it

procrastinate (86): (v.) to delay or postpone action; to put off doing something

procure (13): (v.) to obtain something, usually with effort

proficient (55): (adj.) competent or skilled in doing or using something

profound (22): (adj.) 1. (of a state, quality, or emotion) very great or intense; 2. (concerning a statement or person) having or showing great knowledge or insight

progressive (67): (adj.) 1. developing in stages; proceeding step by step; 2. favoring or implementing social reform or new, liberal ideas

propaganda (77): (n.) information that is typically biased or misleading that is used to promote or publicize a particular political cause or point of view

prose (85): (n.) written or spoken language in its typical form, without metrical structure

provocative (81): (adj.) deliberately evoking annoyance, anger, or another strong reaction; deliberately attempting to arouse sexual desire

prudish (67): (adj.) having the tendency to be easily shocked by matters related to sex or nudity

pugnacious (43): (adj.) eager to argue, quarrel, or fight

putrid (60): (adj.) characteristic of rotting matter and having a foul smell

Q

qualm (31): (n.) an uneasy feeling of doubt, worry, or fear, especially about one's own conduct; a misgiving

quarantine (44): (n.) a state, period, or place of isolation in which people or animals that have arrived from elsewhere or been exposed to infectious or contagious diseases have been placed; (v.) to impose isolation on a person or animal (typically one carrying a disease)

quell (37): (v.) to put an end to rebellion or disorder, usually by force

R

random (45): (adj.) made, done, or chosen without method or conscious thought

ransack (80): (v.) to move hurriedly through a place stealing things and causing damage

ratify (40): (v.) to sign or give formal consent to a law, agreement, or treaty to render it valid

rational (26): (adj.) based on accordance with reason or logic

ravenous (79): (adj.) extremely hungry

realize (36): (v.) 1. to become fully aware of something as fact; 2. to cause something desired or anticipated to happen; 3. to give actual or physical form to an idea or plan; 4. to make money or a profit from a transaction

redress (31): (n.) a remedy or compensation for a wrong or grievance; (v.) to remedy or set right an undesirable situation

reduce (37): (v.) to make or become smaller in size, amount, or degree

reel (6): (n.) a cylinder upon which thread, film, wire, or other materials can be wound; (v.) to feel disoriented, bewildered, or off-kilter from a setback

reform (60): (n.) the action of making changes in something (typically a social, political, or economic institution or practice) in order to improve it (v.) to make changes in something (typically a social, political, or economic institution or practice) in order to improve it

refrain (82): (v.) to stop oneself from doing something

relinquish (18): (v.) to voluntarily give up

reminiscence (20): (n.) a story or recollection of past events

renovate (10): (v.) to restore something old into a good state

replica (67): (n.) an exact copy or model of something, often on a smaller scale

repose (7): (n.) a state of rest, sleep, or tranquility, composure; (v.) to be lying, sitting, or at rest in a particular place

repugnant (64): (adj.) extremely distasteful; unacceptable

repulse (21): (v.) 1. to drive back an attack or an enemy by force; 2. to cause someone to feel intense distaste and aversion

request (46): (n.) an act of asking politely or formally for something; (v.) to ask politely or formally for something

requisition (77): (n.) an official order laying claim to the use of property or materials; (v.) to demand the use or supply of, especially by official order and for military or public use

rescind (16): (v.) to revoke, cancel, or appeal (a law, order, or judgment)

retaliation (25): (n.) the action of returning an attack; a counterattack

revelation (23): (n.) a surprising and previously unknown fact, typically made or revealed in a dramatic way

ridicule (19): (n.) the subjection of someone or something to contemptuous or dismissive language or behavior; (v.) to subject someone or something to contemptuous and dismissive language or behavior

robust (44): (adj.) strong and healthy; vigorous

rotund (15): (adj.) plump; round or spherical

routine (47): (adj.) performed as part of regular procedure; (n.) a sequence of actions regularly followed

rudimentary (39): (adj.) involving or limited to basic principles

ruminate (9): (v.) to think deeply about something

S

sacred (68): (adj.) 1. religious rather than secular; 2. something connected with God or the gods and thus worthy of veneration; 3. regarded with great reverence and respect

sage (73): (adj.) wise; (n.) a profoundly wise (and often old) person

salutation (48): (n.) a gesture or utterance made as a greeting or acknowledgement of another's arrival or departure

sanitary (67): (adj.) of or relating to conditions affecting health or hygiene

savor (7): (v.) to taste, drink, or enjoy something thoroughly and completely

scant (66): (adj.) small or insufficient in quantity or amount

scathing (78): (adj.) severely critical or scornful

seclude (90): (v.) to keep (someone) away from other people

sedate (12): (v.) calm, dignified, and unhurried; quiet and dull

seer (71): (n.) a person who is able to see what the future holds

sentry (71): (n.) a soldier stationed to keep guard over a place

settle (38): (v.) 1. to resolve or reach an agreement an argument or problem; 2. to adopt a more steady and secure lifestyle, usually with a job and a home; 3. to sit or come to rest in a comfortable position

shun (80): (v.) to persistently avoid, ignore, or reject someone or something through antipathy or caution

sluggard (18): (n.) a lazy person

smite (72): (n.) a heavy blow with a weapon or from the hand; (v.) 1. to strike with a firm blow; 2. to affect severely

somber (61): (adj.) dark or dull in color and tone; gloomy

somnolent (77): (adj.) sleepy or drowsy

soothsayer (26): (n.) a person supposedly able to see the future

souvenir (43): (adj.) a thing kept as a reminder of a person, place, or event

sovereign (63): (adj.) possessing supreme or ultimate power; (n.) a supreme ruler, especially a monarch

specter (23): (n.) a ghost

speculate (89): (v.) to form a theory about something without having firm evidence

stamina (58): (n.) the ability to sustain prolonged physical or mental effort

stampede (47): (n.) a sudden panicked rush of a number of horses, cattle, or other animals; (v.) (of horses, cattle, or other animals) to rush wildly in a sudden mass panic

stance (22): (n.) 1. the attitude of a person or organization toward something; 2. the way in which someone stands; posture

stature (34): (n.) 1. a person's natural height; 2.importance or reputation gained by ability or achievement

statute (72): (n.) a written law passed by a legislative body; a rule of an organization or institution

stealthy (20): (adj.) behavior done in a surreptitious manner so as to not be seen or heard

stern (41): (adj.) describing a person who is serious and unrelenting, especially in matters of assertion of authority and exertion of discipline; strict and severe; (n.) the rearmost part of a ship or boat

stifle (81): (v.) to suffocate; to stop one from acting on an emotion; to restrain or prevent

stolid (69): (adj.) characterizing one who is calm and showing little emotion

stupefy (68): (v.) to astonish and shock, often to the point of being unable to think or act properly

sturdy (16): (adj.) strong and solidly built; showing resistance and determination

subdue (61): (v.) to overcome, calm, or bring under control (a feeling or person)

submissive (18): (adj.) ready to conform to the commands or will of others

subsist (13): (v.) to maintain or support oneself, generally at a minimal level

superficial (41): (adj.) existing or occurring on the surface; not thorough, deep, or complete; shallow

swarthy (88): (adj.) dark-skinned

swivel (28): (n.) a coupling between two parts that enables one to revolve about the other; (v.) to turn about a point or axis on a coupling between two parts that enables one to revolve about the other

symbol (14): (n.) a thing that represents or stands for something else, especially a material object that stands for something else

T

taciturn (48): (adj.) a person who is reserved and uncommunicative in speech; saying little

tact (53): (n.) sensitivity in dealing with others or with difficult issues

tailor (70): (n.) a person whose occupation is to adjust clothing (suits, pants, jackets) to fit individual customers; (v.) 1. to make clothes fit individual customers; 2. to make or adapt for a particular purpose or person

tamper (89): (v.) to interfere with something in order to cause damage or make unauthorized alterations

tangible (25): (adj.) 1. perceptible by touch; 2. clear and definite, real

tardy (61): (adj.) delaying or delayed beyond the expected time; late

tedious (10): (adj.) extremely long, slow, or dull; tiresome; monotonous

telepathic (6): (adj.) capable of transmitting thoughts to people without knowing their thoughts; psychic

tempt (15): (v.) to entice; to allure; to try to entice one to do something that he or she finds attractive but that he or she also knows is wrong

tenacious (84): (adj.) tending to keep a firm hold of something; not readily relinquishing a position, principle, or course of action

tentative (82): (adj.) not certain or fixed; provisional

terminate (38): (v.) to bring to an end

terrestrial (53): (adj.) relating to the land or the Earth

texture (12): (n.) the feel, quality, or appearance of a substance or surface; the quality created by a combination of elements in a musical or literary work

thorough (52): (adj.) complete with regard to every detail

token (7): (n.) an object serving as a visible or tangible representation of a fact; a characteristic or distinctive sign or mark of something

tolerate (19): (v.) to allow the existence, practice, or occurrence of something; to be able to withstand something, to endure or accept

tome (13): (n.) a book, particularly one that is large, heavy, and scholarly

tradition (79): (n.) the transmission of customs and beliefs from one generation to the next

transpire (79): (v.) to occur or happen

trepidation (39): (n.) a feeling of fear or agitation about something that may happen

trite (6): (adj.) concerning a remark, opinion, or idea that has lost its import and freshness due to overuse

trivial (58): (adj.) of little value or importance; (of a person) concerned only with trifling or unimportant things

truce (40): (n.) an agreement between enemies or opponents to stop fighting or arguing for a certain time

turbulent (41): (adj.) characterized by conflict, disorder, or confusion; liquid that moves violently and unsteadily

typical (5): (adj.) characteristic of a particular person, thing, group, era, or genre

tyrannical (18): (adj.) exercising power in an arbitrary or cruel way

U

uncanny (41): (adj.) strange or mysterious in an unsettling way

unprecedented (8): (adj.) never done or known before

unswerving (78): (adj.) steady or constant; unchanging or unwavering

untainted (73): (adj.) not contaminated or polluted

upbraid (41): (v.) to scold; to find fault with someone

uphold (31): (v.) to confirm or support something that has happened; to maintain a custom or practice

urge (2): (n.) a strong desire or impulse; (v.) to try to persuade; to recommend strongly; to encourage (an animal or person) to move rapidly or in a certain direction

V

vandalize (49): (v.) to deliberately destroy or damage public or private property

variety (70): (n.) the quality of being different or diverse; the absence of sameness; lacking homogeneity

vehement (36): (adj.) showing strong feeling, especially forceful, passionate, or intense

vent (26): (v.) to give free expression to a strong emotion

veto (23): (v.) a constitutional right to reject a decision or a proposal made by a law-making body

virtuous (36): (adj.) exhibiting high moral standards

void (38): (adj.) 1. not valid or legally binding; 2. completely empty; (n.) a completely empty space; (v.) to declare that something is not valid or legally binding

W

wane (14): (v.) to decrease in vigor or power; to recede; to ebb

whet (4): (v.) 1. to acutely arouse someone's interest in something; 2. to sharpen the blade of an object (usually a knife)

willing (24): (adj.) ready, eager, or prepared to do something

wither (65): (v.) (of a plant) to become dry and shriveled; (of a person) to become shrunken or wrinkled from age or disease; to cease to flourish

withstand (11): (v.) to remain undisturbed or unaffected by something, to resist; to offer strong resistance or opposition to

wound (27): (n.) an injury to living tissue caused by a cut, blow, or other impact; (v.) to inflict an injury on someone

wreak (27): (v.) to inflict a large amount of harm or damage

Y

yearn (57): (v.) to have an intense feeling of longing for something or someone, especially if one is separated from it

Z

zany (11): (adj.) amusingly unconventional and idiosyncratic

zenith (65): (n.) the highest point reached by a celestial or other object

www.ingramcontent.com/pod-product-compliance
Lightning Source LLC
Chambersburg PA
CBHW081425090426
42740CB00017B/3184